The Class of the New ● Richard Barbrook

A Creative Workers in a World City project
Book URL <www.theclassofthenew.net>

Published, POD (print on demand) design and production by
OPENMUTE <openmute.org>

ISBN: 0-9550664-7-6

Copyright

This work is licensed under the Creative Commons Attribution-ShareAlike 2.5 License. To view a copy of this license, visit <creativecommons.org/licenses/by-sa/2.5> or send a letter to Creative Commons, 543 Howard Street, 5th Floor, San Francisco, California, 94105, USA.

Contents

1. Introduction p.007

2. Defining the New Class p.011

3. The Makers of the Future p.015

4. The Classes of the New p.051

5. References p.107

Acknowledgments

Big Shout: Ricardo Ruiz, Tatiana Wells and Paulo Lara for finding and translating Décio Piganatari's definition of the Produsumers.

Respect due: CREAM/University of Westminster; Anthony Iles; Benedict Seymour; Demetra Kotouza; Doug Henwood; John Barker; Ilze Black; Kaveh Nouri; Laura Oldenbourg; Martin Housden; Pauline van Mourik Broekman; Simon Worthington; Sookie Choi; Sonya Williams; Tom Campbell; and the Cybersalon crew.

Soundtrack: Phuture Frequency Radio <www.pfradio.com>.

1.
Introduction

by Anthony Iles & Ben Seymour

In this short book, Richard Barbrook presents a collection of quotations from authors who in different ways attempt to identify an innovative element within society – what Barbrook calls 'the class of the new'. This model workforce announces a new economic and social paradigm, constituting a 'social prophecy' of the shape of work to come. Their mode of being and, in particular, of producing, is set to become hegemonic. No matter how numerically limited at present, the way they live and work today is the way everyone else will live and work tomorrow.

From Adam Smith's 'Philosophers' of the late-eighteenth century, down to the 'Creative Class' celebrated by sociologist Richard Florida today, the class of the new represents the future of production within and, for the author, beyond capitalism. In his essay introducing the textual montage, Barbrook offers his own interpretation of the mutations in the form and content of the class of the new, giving technological development a revelatory role: making new things in new ways constitutes the new class. Marginal at present, it is nonetheless potentially universal.

Focusing on the convergence among ostensibly disparate writers around the notion that contemporary 'immaterial labour' or 'cognitive

The Class of the New

capitalism' is both exemplary and potentially emancipatory, Barbrook considers the claims made for the latest embodiment of the 'class of the new'. If the rhetoric of liberation through new kinds of work is never less than problematic, we should remain optimistic about the tendency of networked, cooperative and 'live-work' forms of production to overturn hierarchies and reduce inequalities in labour and in life. Like the highest stage in the previous orders of technologically-centred development, the class of the new in its current 'creative' and informatic form poses a radical challenge to capitalism's regime of intellectual property and division of labour which could go far beyond what creative class ideologues currently claim for it.

Wagering that this latest incarnation of the class of the new need not remain an exclusive club, Barbrook enjoins the technocrats who oversee the smooth accumulation of capital in 'world cities' like London to consider the economic benefits of including and supporting the 'mass creativity' of those whose work does not yet enjoy the privileged status of 'creative'.

Introduction

Is creativity really becoming the common and decisive feature of all labour? Will securing the increased participation of workers in the 'General Intellect' ensure a smooth transition to communism? Whatever one thinks of Barbrook's own version of the 'social prophecy', he offers penetrating criticisms of the feel good rhetoric of 'Creative Class' boosters such as Florida.

In reality, the numbers may not bear out the great claims made for the Creative Class, whether from the point of view of 'radicals' like Negri and Hardt (who give them a leadership role in the transition beyond Empire) or of those who brandish economic arguments for their supremacy such as Florida. Although both believe that what is good for creatives is now good for capitalism, it is by no means certain that the economic argument for the Creative Class is as strong as its proponents claim.

Focusing on the problems and potential of the latest class of the new in early-twenty-first century London, an environment where the conditions for its triumph are purportedly most promising, this book gives much needed historical and social context to current debates around 'cognitive capitalism' and the transformation of work it is said to entail.

2.
Defining the New Class

- The Philosophers – Adam Smith (1776) ... p.051
- The Industrials – Henri Saint-Simon (1819) ... p.052
- The Civil Servants – Georg Hegel (1821) ... p.053
- The Bohemians – Adolphe d'Ennery and Grangé (1843) ... p.053
- The Bourgeoisie – Karl Marx and Friedrich Engels (1848) ... p.054
- The General Intellect – Karl Marx (1857) ... p.054
- The Self-Made Man – Samuel Smiles (1859) ... p.055
- The Labour Movement – Karl Marx (1867) ... p.055
- The Educated Working Man – Thomas Wright (1868) ... p.056
- The Superman – Friedrich Nietzsche (1883) ... p.057
- The Aristocracy of the Working Class – Friedrich Engels (1885) ... p.058
- The New Middle Class – William Morris (1885) ... p.058
- The Intellectual Proletariat – William Morris (1888) ... p.059
- The Vanguard Party – V.I. Lenin (1902) ... p.059
- The Samurai – H.G. Wells (1905) ... p.060

The Class of the New

- The Bureaucrats – Max Weber (1910) ... p.060
- The Scientific Managers – Frederick Winslow Taylor (1911) ... p.060
- The Labour Aristocracy – V.I. Lenin (1916) ... p.061
- The Labour Bureaucracy – Gregory Zinoviev (1916) ... p.061
- The Blackshirts – Mario Piazzesi (1921) ... p.062
- The Engineers – Thorstein Veblen (1921) ... p.062
- The Fordist Worker – Henry Ford (1922) ... p.063
- The Open Conspiracy – H.G. Wells (1928) ... p.064
- The Intellectuals – Antonio Gramsci (1934) ... p.065
- The Managerial Class – James Burnham (1941) ... p.065
- The Entrepreneurs – Joseph Schumpeter (1942) ... p.066
- The Inner Party – George Orwell (1948) ... p.066
- The New Middle Class – C. Wright Mills (1951) ... p.067
- The Power Elite – C. Wright Mills (1956) ... p.067
- The Organisation Man – William Whyte (1956) ... p.068
- The New Class – Milovan Djilas (1957) ... p.069
- The Specialists – Ralf Dahrendorf (1957) ... p.069
- The New Class – J.K. Galbraith (1958) ... p.070
- The Industrial Managers – Clark Kerr (1960) ... p.070
- The Order-Givers – Cornelius Castoriadis (1961) ... p.071
- The New Working Class – Serge Mallet (1963) ... p.072
- The Knowledge Workers – Peter Drucker (1966) ... p.072
- The Educational and Scientific Estate – J.K. Galbraith (1967) ... p.073
- The Technocrats – Alain Touraine (1969) ... p.074
- The Hippies – Abbie Hoffman and Jerry Rubin (1969) ... p.074
- The Produsumers – Décio Piganatari (1969) ... p.075
- The Scientific Intellectual Labourers – Ernest Mandel (1972) ... p.076
- The Knowledge Class – Daniel Bell (1973) ... p.077
- The Intermediate Layers – Harry Braverman (1974) ... p.078
- The New Petty-Bourgeoisie – Nicos Poulantzas (1974) ... p.079
- The Professional-Managerial Class – Barbara & John Ehrenreich (1975) ... p.079
- The Proletarianised Professionals – Stanley Aronowitz (1975) ... p.080

Defining the New Class

- The Post-Modernists – Jean-François Lyotard (1979) ... p.081
- The Socialised Workers – Antonio Negri (1980) ... p.082
- The White-Collar Proletarians – Michael Kelly (1980) ... p.083
- The Nomads – Gilles Deleuze and Félix Guattari (1980) ... p.083
- The Prosumers – Alvin & Heidi Toffler (1980) ... p.084
- The Post-Industrial Proletarians – André Gorz (1980) ... p.085
- The Entrepreneurs – George Gilder (1981) ... p.086
- The Venture Capitalists – John Naisbitt (1982) ... p.087
- The Hackers – Steven Levy (1984) ... p.088
- The Cyborgs – Donna Haraway (1985) ... p.088
- The Symbolic Analysts – Robert Reich (1991) ... p.089
- The Virtual Class – Arthur Kroker and Michael Weinstein (1994) ... p.090
- The Netizens – Michael & Ronda Hauben (1995) ... p.090
- The Digerati – John Brockman (1996) ... p.091
- The Multipreneurs – Tom Gorman (1996) ... p.091
- The Immaterial Labourers – Maurizio Lazzarato (1996) ... p.092
- The Digital Artisans – Richard Barbrook and Pit Schultz (1997) ... p.093
- The Digital Citizen – Jon Katz (1997) ... p.094
- The Swarm Capitalists – Kevin Kelly (1998) ... p.094
- The New Independents – Charlie Leadbeater and Kate Oakley (1999) ... p.095
- The Elancers – Helen Wilkinson (1999) ... p.096
- The Multitude – Antonio Negri and Michael Hardt (2000) ... p.096
- The New Barbarians – Ian Angell (2000) ... p.097
- The Bobos (Bourgeois Bohemians) – David Brooks (2000) ... p.097
- The Cognitariat – Franco Bifo Berardi (2001) ... p.098
- The Free Agents – Daniel Pink (2001) ... p.099
- The Cybertariat – Ursula Huws (2001) ... p.100
- The Netocracy – Alexander Bard and Jan Söderqvist (2002) ... p.100
- The Precariat – Frassanito Network (2002) ... p.101
- The Creative Class – Richard Florida (2002) ... p.102
- The Pro-Ams – Charlie Leadbeater and Paul Miller (2004) ... p.103

3.
The Makers of the Future

If the previous decades have been the years of the management consultants, the next decades may be the years of the designers, publishers, artists and a variety of other [creative] skills.[1]

Ken Livingstone, Mayor of London.

The economy of England's capital city is once again undergoing a dramatic transformation. In 2002, the GLA (Greater London Authority) published a report which identified the creative industries as – after business services – the locality's fastest growing sector of wealth production and employment opportunities. Its authors explained that – just like their forebears who moved from the artisan's workshop to the Fordist factory – the present generation of Londoners are learning how to make new things in new ways with new technologies. If the city was to prosper over the next few decades, the Mayor's economic strategy must be focused on providing support and encouragement

---

[1] GLA Economics, *Creativity*, page 3.

The Class of the New

for the businesses of the future: 'advertising; architecture; the art and antiques market; crafts; design; designer fashion; film and video; interactive leisure software; music; the performing arts; publishing; software and computer services; and television and radio.'[2]

For Ken Livingstone, fostering the creative industries is also electorally advantageous. His victory as the Labour candidate in the 2004 Mayoral contest demonstrated that the growth of this sector was widening the voting base for progressive politics in London. Richard Florida's *The Rise of the Creative Class* has provided the GLA with a theoretical explanation of this shift in party loyalties. According to the findings of his research, the new employers of the information age require a new type of employee: highly educated, culturally aware and technologically adept. As the experience of American cities has proved, tolerance, diversity and eccentricity are the preconditions for attracting the members of the Creative Class whose skills and inventiveness are vital for economic prosperity. In an ironic twist, conservative attitudes are now seen as bad for business.[3]

For those of a more sceptical disposition, Florida's analysis is far too one-sided. When applied to London, his celebration of the creative industries minimises – and excuses – the downsides of the restructuring of the city's economy: the dominance of international finance, the casualisation of employment and the gentrification of working class neighbourhoods.[4] Some observers have even questioned whether the growth of the knowledge economy has changed the exploitative structures of capitalism in any significant way. In the 2000s, an oligopoly of large corporations and big banks still rules the world.[5] Despite the cogency of their criticisms, these dissenters have remained a minority voice. Far from rejecting Florida's approach, the most influential thinkers on both the Right and the Left are promoting their own versions of the Creative Class. Just like him, they're also convinced that the new economic paradigm will vindicate their

---

[2] GLA Economics, *Creativity*, page 5.//
[3] See Richard Florida, *The Rise of the Creative Class*, pages 215-314.//
[4] See David Panos, 'Create Creative Clusters'; and Benedict Seymour, 'Shoreditch and the Creative Destruction of the Inner City'.//
[5] See Aufheben, 'Keep on Smiling'.

own political stance. According to taste, the growth in the number of information workers can be interpreted as the imminent triumph of either dotcom capitalism or cybernetic communism. Although often bitterly divided in their politics, these gurus still share a common theoretical position. Whether on the Right or the Left, all of them champion the same social prophecy: the new class is prefiguring today how everyone else will work and live tomorrow.

Their theoretical analyses have a venerable pedigree. Long before the Creative Class became a fashionable phrase, the members of this new social group were being described as the Prosumers, the Venture Capitalists, the Cyborgs and the Symbolic Analysts. Back in the early-1970s, Daniel Bell formulated the theoretical template for this social prophecy. Inspired by Marshall McLuhan's technological reveries, he claimed that the rapid convergence of media, telecommunications and computing was sweeping away the economic, political and cultural certainties of the industrial age. Anticipating universal access to the Net, Bell predicted that the advent of the information society would inevitably lead to the hegemony of the creators of information: the Knowledge Class.[6] Over three decades have passed since this prophecy was first made. The terminology may have changed many times and its political meaning taken different forms, but the theory has remained the same. The rapid spread and increasing sophistication of the Net is bringing about the rise to power of the Knowledge Class. The future is what it used to be.[7]

In the early-twenty-first century, analysts and intellectuals are still entranced by this McLuhanist vision of the new class. Across the political spectrum, the Net is praised as the demiurge of the hegemony of the producers of information. Yet, for all its futurist rhetoric, the theoretical antecedents of this prophecy can be traced back even further than Bell's speculations in the early-1970s. At the dawn of modernity in the late-eighteenth century, Adam Smith was the first person to put forward the argument that the economic growth was creating a specific group of modernisers. By deepening the division of labour,

---

[6] See Daniel Bell, *The Coming of Post-Industrial Society*.

[7] For a more detailed analysis of the historical origins of the information society prophecy, see Richard Barbrook, *Imaginary Futures*.

the market and the factory were increasing the efficiency of the workforce and raising the quality of their products.[8] Within an economy diversified into different specialist trades, the Philosophers who improved and invented machinery had acquired a distinctive social role: designing the future.

In the more than two centuries which have passed between Adam Smith's time and our own, many different thinkers have proposed their own versions of the theory of the new class. Following the examples of Walter Benjamin's *The Arcades Project* and Humphrey Jennings' *Pandaemonium*, the next section of this book uses a montage of quotations to tell the story of this social prophecy. In the same way that music samples can be mixed together to make a new tune, Benjamin discovered that his collection of research notes was turning into a book in its own right. Just like splicing different shots together to produce a film, Jennings constructed a historical narrative out of quotations from many different authors. What intrigued Benjamin was that this approach was able to reveal the contemporary 'after-life' of writings from the past. Creating a montage of quotations could achieve what he believed to be the primary purpose of historical research: understanding what was happening in the present. For Jennings, this technique allowed his readers to experience the cultural and political complexity of the past. By presenting the divergent views of our forebears, he could show that there was nothing preordained about the social structures of the present. Collecting quotations was his poetic antidote to the positivist certainties of academic historians.[9]

Inspired by Benjamin and Jennings' methodology, this book brings together 86 definitions of the new class from the past 230 years. The well-known passages by famous authors are included along with obscure pieces by long-forgotten writers. The seekers after wisdom are found side-by-side with the promoters of confusion. Of course, the quotations which have been chosen are only short excerpts from long books. Because the passages were selected for their relevance to the overall argument of this book, the more nuanced positions of their

---

[8] See Adam Smith, *The Wealth of Nations Volume 1*, pages 7-25.
[9] See Walter Benjamin, *The Arcades Project*, page 456-476; and Humphrey Jennings, *Pandaemonium*, pages xxxv-xxxix.

authors are often lost. There is no substitute for reading the original texts. Yet, as Benjamin and Jennings demonstrated, a montage of quotations will create its own meanings. Reading through these different concepts of the class of the new reveals both continuities and discontinuities in the definition of this icon of modernity over the last two centuries. By analysing what has changed and what has remained the same, we can come closer to comprehending the political and economic significance of this social prophecy in the present.

The process of selecting quotations for this book highlights what thinkers with very different ideological positions have in common. Whatever their political loyalties, their definitions of the new class all start from the same fundamental theoretical insight: human history is an evolutionary process. In agrarian societies, time was seen as cyclical and immutable. Both Aristotle and Muhammad Ibn Khaldûn analysed history as the repetitive rise and fall of the same contending classes.[10] But, with the advent of modernity, time became the linear movement of progress. In *The Wealth of Nations*, Adam Smith explained that humanity had evolved through a succession of economic stages: hunting, herding, agriculture and, finally, commerce.[11] Crucially, it was this materialist conception of history which inspired his characterisation of the Philosophers as the class of the new. If agriculture had evolved into commerce, then capitalism itself must also be a dynamic social system. The inventors of machinery were the makers of the future.

From Adam Smith's first iteration, all subsequent definitions of the new class have derived their theoretical foundation: historical evolution. Like Benjamin and Jennings, many of the promoters of this concept on the Left have also been sceptical about the benefits of capitalist progress. However, this rejection of Adam Smith's economic liberalism didn't lead them into sociological Creationism. On the contrary, they saw the new class as the promise of a new – and better – society. Just as importantly, the intellectuals of the Right never used

---

[10] See Aristotle, *The Politics*, pages 101-234; and Muhammad Ibn Khaldûn, *The Mugaddimah*, pages 91-261.

[11] See Adam Smith, *The Wealth of Nations Volume 1*, pages 401-445; *Volume 2*, pages 213-253. Also see Adam Ferguson, *An Essay on the History of Civil Society*.

The Class of the New

this theory to advocate a return to the agrarian past. When Friedrich Nietzsche proclaimed the advent of the Superman in the 1880s, his aristocratic fantasy was presented as a modernist alternative to the equalitarian path of social evolution. According to Mario Piazzesi, the chronicler of the fascist counter-revolution in 1920s Italy, the Blackshirts were hi-tech warriors and businessmen. In more recent times, Ian Angell has promoted the concept of the New Barbarians while Alexander Bard and Jan Söderqvist have looked forward to the ascendancy of the Netocracy. Echoing Nietzsche, these conservatives argued that – far from being retrogressive – their elitist dreams described the inevitable consequences of historical progress. The only way of restoring feudal privileges is moving forwards into the future.

For each and every one of the authors in this book, defining the new class was a way of describing their own experience of the evolution of capitalism. Over the past two centuries, the restructuring of working methods and the development of better machinery have been the driving forces of this economic system.[12] Each wave of organisational and technological changes has required another reordering of the hierarchical relationship between capital and labour.[13] In successive generations, the concept of the new class has been used to analyse the impact of this process upon the social structures of modernity. The majority of the definitions in this book were attempts to understand how the latest surge of progress was going to impact upon the opposing poles of the capitalist economy. Depending upon the political motivations of their authors, the concepts of the class of the new have taken two distinct forms: the new ruling class and the new working class. Sometimes the same definition has been used to identify the latest iteration of both capital and labour. In other cases, different concepts have described the new forms of a specific class. By assigning them to one or both of these variants, the definitions of the new class form two distinctive lines of historical succession:

---

[12] See Karl Marx, *Grundrisse*, pages 690-743; *Capital Volume 1*, pages 492-639, 1034-1065.

[13] See the analyses of the changing social composition of the twentieth century European and American class systems in Sergio Bologna, 'The Tribe of Moles'; and Antonio Negri, 'Keynes and the Capitalist Theories of the State Post-1929'.

The New Ruling Class
the Philosophers ⅠⅠ▶ the Industrials ⅠⅠ▶ the Civil Servants ⅠⅠ▶ the Bourgeoisie ⅠⅠ▶ the Self-Made Man ⅠⅠ▶ the Superman ⅠⅠ▶ the Vanguard Party ⅠⅠ▶ the Samurai ⅠⅠ▶ the Bureaucrats ⅠⅠ▶ the Scientific Managers ⅠⅠ▶ the Blackshirts ⅠⅠ▶ the Open Conspiracy ⅠⅠ▶ the Intellectuals ⅠⅠ▶ the Managerial Class ⅠⅠ▶ the Entrepreneurs ⅠⅠ▶ the Inner Party ⅠⅠ▶ the Power Elite ⅠⅠ▶ the New Class ⅠⅠ▶ the Industrial Managers ⅠⅠ▶ the Order-Givers ⅠⅠ▶ the Technocrats ⅠⅠ▶ the Knowledge Class ⅠⅠ▶ the Post-Modernists ⅠⅠ▶ the Professional-Managerial Class ⅠⅠ▶ the Entrepreneurs ⅠⅠ▶ the Venture Capitalists ⅠⅠ▶ the Symbolic Analysts ⅠⅠ▶ the Virtual Class ⅠⅠ▶ the Digerati ⅠⅠ▶ the Digital Citizen ⅠⅠ▶ the Swarm Capitalists ⅠⅠ▶ the New Barbarians ⅠⅠ▶ the Bobos ⅠⅠ▶ the Netocracy ⅠⅠ▶ the Creative Class.

The New Working Class
the Industrials ⅠⅠ▶ the Bohemians ⅠⅠ▶ the General Intellect ⅠⅠ▶ the Labour Movement ⅠⅠ▶ the Educated Working Man ⅠⅠ▶ the Aristocracy of the Working Class ⅠⅠ▶ the Intellectual Proletariat ⅠⅠ▶ the Vanguard Party ⅠⅠ▶ the Labour Aristocracy ⅠⅠ▶ the Engineers ⅠⅠ▶ the Fordist Worker ⅠⅠ▶ the Intellectuals ⅠⅠ▶ the New Working Class ⅠⅠ▶ the Knowledge Workers ⅠⅠ▶ the Educational and Scientific Estate ⅠⅠ▶ the Hippies ⅠⅠ▶ the Produsumers ⅠⅠ▶ the Scientific Intellectual Labourers ⅠⅠ▶ the Proletarianised Professionals ⅠⅠ▶ the Post-Modernists ⅠⅠ▶ the Socialised Workers ⅠⅠ▶ the White-Collar Proletarians ⅠⅠ▶ the Nomads ⅠⅠ▶ the Prosumers ⅠⅠ▶ the Post-Industrial Proletarians ⅠⅠ▶ the Hackers ⅠⅠ▶ the Cyborgs ⅠⅠ▶ the Symbolic Analysts ⅠⅠ▶ the Virtual Class ⅠⅠ▶ the Netizens ⅠⅠ▶ the Multipreneurs ⅠⅠ▶ the Immaterial Labourers ⅠⅠ▶ the Digital Artisans ⅠⅠ▶ the New Independents ⅠⅠ▶ the Elancers ⅠⅠ▶ the Multitude ⅠⅠ▶ the Cognitariat ⅠⅠ▶ the Free Agents ⅠⅠ▶ the Cybertariat ⅠⅠ▶ the Precariat ⅠⅠ▶ the Creative Class ⅠⅠ▶ the Pro-Ams.

These two parallel histories demonstrate how – as Benjamin and Jennings pointed out – a montage of quotations can reveal its own meanings. By following the two lines of succession, it becomes clear that the originators of these different versions of the new class were responding to the evolution of the capitalist economy. In its early liberal form, the leaders of the emerging industrial system were lauded as heroic and innovative individuals: the Philosophers, the Industrials, the Self-Made Man and the Superman. Even the socialist critics of capitalism could admire the dynamism of the new class of the Bourgeoisie which '... has created more massive and colossal productive forces than have all preceding generations together.'[14] Facing this formidable enemy, the Left argued that the proletariat was also one of the primary driving forces of modernity: the Industrials, the Bohemians, the General Intellect, the Labour Movement, the Educated Working Man and the Aristocracy of the Working Class.

As liberalism gave way to Fordism, the dominant archetype of the new class changed almost beyond recognition.[15] For the analysts of the elite, their most pressing task was to name the bosses who ran the rapidly expanding bureaucracies of big business and big government. Already, in the early-nineteenth century, Georg Hegel had anticipated this new form of the new ruling class in his concept of the Civil Servants. Inspired by this example, twentieth century thinkers produced a plethora of definitions for the rulers of Fordism: the Samurai, the Bureaucrats, the Scientific Managers, the Blackshirts, the Open Conspiracy, the Managerial Class, the Power Elite, the Industrial Managers, the Order-Givers, the Technocrats and the Professional-Managerial Class. Instead of opposing the rise of this administrative elite, some groups on the Left seized this opportunity to turn themselves into the masters of the bureaucratic system. Inspired by the Fabians' statist redefinition of socialism, H.G. Wells argued that the Samurai had replaced the Labour Movement as the pioneer of the post-capitalist future. The tragedy of the 1917 Russian revolution – when the leadership of the oppressed became their oppressors – can be followed through the different definitions of this specific type of the new ruling class: the Vanguard Party, the Labour Bureaucracy, the Intellectuals, the Inner Party and Milovan Djilas' version of the New Class.

According to Henry Ford himself, the Fordist Worker – the employees of the factories which epitomised the bureaucratisation of capitalism – was the sort of person who '... wants a job in which he does not have to think.'[16] Ironically, although he gave his name to this economic paradigm, this captain of industry's definition ignored one of the most

---

[14] Karl Marx and Friedrich Engels, *The Communist Manifesto*, page 20.

[15] For an explanation of this transformation of capitalism, see Michel Aglietta, *A Theory of Capitalist Regulation*.

[16] Henry Ford, *My Life and Work*, page 103.

distinctive features of corporate capitalism: the proletarianisation of scientific, technical, administrative and intellectual labour. From the late-nineteenth century onwards, influential social theorists have emphasised the prefigurative role of this group of educated and cultured employees. Far from producing a population of mindless drones, Fordism was creating its own bureaucratic versions of the new working class: the Intellectual Proletariat, the Vanguard Party, the Labour Aristocracy, the Engineers, the Intellectuals, the New Working Class, the Knowledge Workers, the Educational and Scientific Estate, the Scientific Intellectual Labourers, the Proletarianised Professionals and the White-Collar Proletarians.

When Fordism was superseded, there was another dramatic shift in the dominant archetype of this social prophecy. The evolution of the economy required a rethinking of fundamental ideas. In the mid-twentieth century, Joseph Schumpeter was already arguing for a new vision of the new ruling class: the Entrepreneurs. Dismissed at the time as nostalgia for the liberal icon of the Self-Made Man, his concept provided the inspiration four decades later for a new generation of conservative thinkers in America and Europe who had lost faith in the infallibility of big business and big government. Throughout the 1980s, they proclaimed the imminent triumph of a heroic elite of innovators, fortune hunters and speculators: George Gilder's definition of the Entrepreneurs and the Venture Capitalists. Above all, like Adam Smith, these theorists argued that the transformative power of new technology was behind the rise of this new ruling class. From the early-1990s onwards, as media, telecommunications and computing converged into the Net, the charismatic leaders of hi-tech businesses were praised as the makers of the future: the Symbolic Analysts, the Virtual Class, the Digerati, the Digital Citizen, the Swarm Capitalists, the New Barbarians, the Bobos, the Netocracy and the Creative Class.

The faltering of Fordism also tarnished the modernist image of the new working class of salaried intellectuals employed by the large corporations and government departments. At first, the young people radicalised in the 1960s sought a replacement for this social group among their peers who – like the Bohemians in the early-nineteenth century – were looking for a way of living outside the confines of the bureaucratic system: the Hippies, the Produsumers, the Post-Modernists and the Nomads. But, as the crisis of Fordism deepened,

The Class of the New

the economic consequences of the restructuring of capitalism could no longer be ignored. Crucially, it was the refusal of many young workers to conform to the disciplines of the factory and the office which had discredited bureaucratic methods of organisation. In the late-1970s and early-1980s, some theorists argued that economic changes were building the political base of the New Left revolution. The growth in self-employment and short-term contracts was creating a new – and fiercely independent – working class: the Socialised Workers and the Post-Industrial Proletarians.

During the 1990s, this radical prophecy became a mainstream orthodoxy. What was once denounced as New Left subversion was now praised as neo-liberal modernisation. In the fashionable business manuals of the dotcom boom, top-down bureaucracy was castigated as an expensive and inefficient method of controlling the labour force of the information economy.[17] Three decades earlier, Peter Drucker – the founding father of management theory – had pointed out that: 'The knowledge worker cannot be supervised closely or in detail … he must direct himself.'[18] Building upon this analysis, his admirers explained that the new post-Fordist working class was quite capable of managing its own exploitation by capital: the Multipreneurs, the New Independents, the Elancers, the Free Agents and the Pro-Ams. From the early-1980s onwards, the growth of this self-directed form of employment was closely associated with the accelerating convergence of media, telecommunications and computing. In their definitions, some intellectuals have emphasised the benefits that this new entrepreneurial working class derives from the knowledge economy: the Prosumers, the Hackers, the Symbolic Analysts, the Virtual Class, the Digital Citizen and the Creative Class. Others have celebrated the subversive potential of the networked proletariat: the Cyborgs, the Netizens, the Immaterial Labourers, the Digital Artisans, the Multitude, the Cognitariat, the Cybertariat and the Precariat. Above all, whether they were on the Right or the Left, these analysts insisted that the new working class of this cognitive stage of capitalism should

---

[17] See Rick Levine, Christopher Locke, Doc Searls and David Weinberger, *The Cluetrain Manifesto*; and Jonas Ridderstråle and Kjell Nordström, *Funky Business*.

[18] Peter Drucker, *The Effective Executive*, page 4.

be admired for its intellectual accomplishments, cultural sophistication and technological savvy.[19]

This contemporary fascination with the educated and entrepreneurial members of the proletariat has deep historical roots. For over two centuries, creativity has been at the centre of the struggle between capital and labour. As the industrial system has evolved, the contending classes have fought not only over the division of the fruits of production, but also over the control of the workplace. In *The Wealth of Nations*, Adam Smith showed how the increasing division of labour allowed capitalists to replace self-governing skilled artisans with more submissive unskilled employees.[20] In *Capital*, Karl Marx explained how the introduction of more advanced machinery enabled factory managers to determine the pace and intensity of work.[21] During the first half of the twentieth century, this separation of conception and action reached its apogee. Frederick Winslow Taylor believed that the Scientific Managers could monopolise all decision-making within the economy. Henry Ford offered higher wages in return for the Fordist Worker submitting unquestioningly to the disciplines of the assembly line. In the early-twentieth century, even prominent anti-capitalist intellectuals were convinced that this division between thinking and doing was not only inevitable, but also desirable. Just like the Scientific Managers within the factories, V.I. Lenin argued that the Vanguard Party should become the absolute master of the political organisations of the Left. In the same way that the Bureaucrats dominated their offices, H.G. Wells believed that the Open Conspiracy could impose order and discipline upon unstable market economies. For the followers of all of these sages, the rise of big business and big government during the mid-twentieth century seemed like the fulfilment of their authoritarian prophecies of a new ruling class which decided everything lording over a new working class which decided nothing. At the high-point of Fordism, Cornelius Castoriadis summarised the essence of this economic paradigm: 'The

---

[19] For an analysis of this transition, see Carlo Vercellone, 'Sens et Enjeux de la Transition vers le Capitalisme Cognitif'.

[20] See Adam Smith, *The Wealth of Nations Volume 1*, pages 7-25.

[21] See Karl Marx, *Capital Volume 1*, pages 553-564.

The Class of the New

increasing bureaucratisation of all social activities ... [means] the division of society into order-givers and order-takers.'[22]

The catalyst of the next evolutionary leap of capitalism was the late-1960s New Left rebellion against this absolute separation between conception and action. By proletarianising intellectual labour, Fordism had created a dissident minority within the workforce who were no longer willing to abdicate their right to think in return for the rewards of consumer society.[23] For the past forty years, the advocates of new definitions of the new ruling class and the new working class have been trying to describe the implications of this momentous shift in attitudes. On the Right, thinkers have claimed that the decline of Fordism has opened up the opportunity for everyone to become a member of the elite. Around the same time that Schumpeter was elaborating his thesis, Friedrich Hayek and Ludwig von Mises – the gurus of neo-liberalism – were stressing that the most important activity of the Entrepreneurs was 'discovery': making better use of scarce resources to improve the choice, quality and affordability of products within the marketplace.[24] Inspired by this analysis, conservative thinkers in the 1980s and 1990s argued that the rigid divisions between employers and employees were disappearing in the post-Fordist economy. From San Francisco to London, the same nostrums were promulgated.[25] With a good idea and a bit of luck, any worker could found a thriving dotcom business and become a successful member of the Digerati. Whether they were Symbolic Analysts or Free Agents, individuals were now responsible for their own destinies in the unregulated global marketplace. Freed from bureaucratic diktats, both the Bobos and the Digital Citizens were able to express their own opinions and experiment with new ideas. Above all, in the age of the Net, economic dynamism depended upon lavishly rewarding the hi-tech Entrepreneurs. According to Gilder, the lessons of history were clear: 'Material progress is ineluctably elitist ...

---

[22] Paul Cardan [Cornelius Castoriadis], *Modern Capitalism and Revolution*, page 3.

[23] See Alain Lipietz, *Towards a New Economic Order*, pages 14-23; and Antonio Negri, 'Archaeology and Project'.

[24] See Friedrich Hayek, *Individualism and Economic Order*, pages 33-56, 77-118; and Ludwig von Mises, *Human Action*, pages 251-256, 327-350.

[25] See Richard Barbrook and Andy Cameron, 'The Californian Ideology'.

exalting the few extraordinary men who can produce wealth over the democratic masses who consume it.'[26]

For all its post-Fordist rhetoric, this neo-liberal celebration of the Entrepreneurs perpetuated the Fordist assumption that the new ruling class monopolised the making of the future. In a tautological argument, whenever workers demonstrated any autonomy, inventiveness or initiative, they were deemed to be behaving just like members of the elite: the Symbolic Analysts, the Virtual Class, the Multipreneurs, the New Independents, the Elancers, the Free Agents and the Creative Class. This confusion about the social status of these self-directed and self-motivated employees was partially a form of ideological mystification which rebranded market disciplines and job insecurity as individual freedom and career opportunities. Yet, at the same time, these definitions of the new working class were also genuine attempts to grasp the implications of the waning of Fordism. In contrast to the rigid hierarchies of this mid-twentieth century form of capitalism, the educational and cultural dividing lines between employers and employees in the knowledge economy have become much less distinct. The self-exploiting Digital Artisans had the same tastes, obsessions and lifestyles as the Swarm Capitalists who exploited them. As Ursula Huws pointed out, the corporate bosses who were reliant upon the technological expertise of the Cybertariat to operate their own computers couldn't pretend to be the fount of all wisdom. David Brooks was amused that the rise of the Bobos – bourgeois bohemians – proved that the 1960s New Left might have lost the economic argument, but the Hippies had won the cultural war. When there was no longer an unbridgeable gulf between the order-givers and the order-takers, the same definition of the new class could easily be used to describe both the new ruling class and the new working class. Crucially, by covering both opposing poles of the capitalist economy, these thinkers were able to revive another potent form of this social prophecy: the class of the new as the new intermediate class. As with its two other forms, this third variant can also be tracked as the historical succession of different definitions:

---

[26] George Gilder, *Wealth and Poverty*, page 273.

The New Intermediate Class

the Industrials ▸ the Bohemians ▸ the New Middle Class ▸ the Bureaucrats ▸ the Labour Aristocracy ▸ the Labour Bureaucracy ▸ the Engineers ▸ the Intellectuals ▸ the New Middle Class ▸ the Organisation Man ▸ the Specialists ▸ the New Class ▸ the Educational and Scientific Estate ▸ the Produsumers ▸ the Scientific Intellectual Labourers ▸ the Knowledge Class ▸ the Intermediate Layers ▸ the New Petty-Bourgeoisie ▸ the Post-Modernists ▸ the Nomads ▸ the Prosumers ▸ the Hackers ▸ the Symbolic Analysts ▸ the Virtual Class ▸ the Netizens ▸ the Multipreneurs ▸ the Digital Artisans ▸ the Digital Citizen ▸ the New Independents ▸ the Elancers ▸ the Multitude ▸ the Bobos ▸ the Free Agents ▸ the Creative Class ▸ the Pro-Ams.

In the first phase of capitalist development, Henri Saint-Simon had pioneered this interpretation of the new class by including both employers and employees within his definition of the Industrials. Whatever divided them inside the factory, these two groups had a common interest in displacing the parasitic aristocracy and clergy which had dominated the agrarian economy. But, within a generation, his socialist followers had become convinced that Saint-Simon's concept of an all-embracing class of the new was an anachronism. In *The Communist Manifesto*, Karl Marx and Friedrich Engels predicted that economic modernisation would not only sweep away the old feudal order, but also deepen the social divisions within capitalism. As competition intensified, artisans would be driven out of business, self-employed professionals would be forced to work for wages and peasants would lose their land.[27] Far from resisting this path of progress, the primary task of the new class of the Labour Movement was campaigning for reforms like the Factory Acts which – by raising wages and improving conditions – accelerated the polarisation of society into the ever-diminishing minority who owned the hi-tech factories and the ever-expanding majority who worked in them. At the end of this evolutionary process, when almost the entire population had been proletarianised, the working class would be reborn as the new directing force of modernity: the General Intellect.

---

[27] See Karl Marx and Friedrich Engels, *The Communist Manifesto*, pages 21-35.

During the late-nineteenth century and early-twentieth century, this Marxist analysis provided a distinctive ideological identity for the increasingly powerful parliamentary socialist parties and industrial trade unions in Europe. Their day-to-day struggles for reforms within capitalism were inevitably leading to the revolutionary moment of communist emancipation.[28] As liberalism evolved into Fordism, social democrats argued that Marx's predictions were being realised as the number of wage-earners grew and the corporatisation of the economy gathered pace. Not surprisingly, their opponents across the political spectrum – including some who described themselves as Marxists – were anxious to provide their own alternative explanations of the evolutionary direction of capitalism. Rejecting Marx's thesis that modernity was the progressive polarisation of society into two distinct classes, these thinkers focused upon the intermediate groups within the economy which couldn't be classified as either part of the bourgeoisie or the proletariat. They were delighted to discover that – even in the mid-twentieth century economies dominated by big business and big government – a substantial proportion of the population still made their living as artisans, self-employed professionals and peasants.[29]

More importantly, since these sectors were undergoing a long-term decline, the critics of Marx were also able to identify a more modern form of the intermediate class. Ironically, the proletarianisation of intellectual labour had created the conditions for the emergence of this group positioned between the bourgeoisie and the proletariat. Unlike the Fordist Workers on the assembly-line, this new intermediate class hadn't surrendered all of its autonomy to the Scientific Managers and their machinery. Although these wage-earners might not have owned capital, members of this privileged group did possess other potent sources of economic power: educational qualifications and cultural knowledge. Across the political spectrum, thinkers championed their different versions of the new intermediate class. For moderates, the robustness of capitalism had been proved. Instead of social polarisation, economic modernisation was creating the living embodiment of consensus and compromise: C. Wright

---

[28] See Karl Kautsky, *The Class Struggle*.

[29] See Ralf Dahrendorf, *Class and Class Conflict in an Industrial Society*, pages 136-141; and Nicos Poulantzas, *Classes in Contemporary Capitalism*, pages 285-286, 328-331.

The Class of the New

Mill's New Middle Class, the Organisation Man, the Specialists and J.K. Galbraith's New Class. For revolutionaries, the growth of the new intermediate class confirmed the political indispensability of the Vanguard Party. Far from uniting the population into the General Intellect, the evolution of capitalism was spawning privileged minorities which perpetuated the divisions within the exploited masses: William Morris' New Middle Class, the Labour Aristocracy, the Labour Bureaucracy, the Intellectuals, the Educational and Scientific Estate, the Scientific Intellectual Labourers, the Intermediate Layers and the New Petty-Bourgeoisie. Whatever their political motivations, all of these intellectuals were convinced that the only variant of the new class which explained the unique social structure of industrial capitalism was the new intermediate class.

As Fordism evolved into post-Fordism, this strand of the social prophecy also had to abandon its bureaucratic archetype. Looking for a replacement, intellectuals turned to the canonical texts of McLuhanism. If the convergence of media, telecommunications and computing was the demiurge of social change, then the builders of the Net must be the cutting-edge of modernity. In the knowledge economy, all definitions of the new intermediate class have to be an updated version of the Knowledge Class. During the 1990s, the third variant of the social prophecy flourished among the analysts of the rapid and chaotic expansion of the dotcom sector. In the new paradigm of the new economy, the educated and entrepreneurial employees of the new media companies were praised as pioneers of a new version of the new intermediate class. Looking at their working patterns and cultural attitudes, they couldn't be easily identified as either strictly bourgeois or proletarian. The New Independents and the Free Agents moved from short-term contract jobs to running up their own companies and back again. The Netizens and the Bobos dressed in the same clothes, drank in the same bars, listened to the same music and shared a common obsession with cutting-edge technology. Above all, both the Digital Artisans and the Digital Citizens believed that the measure of success wasn't just making lots of money, but also creating something cool.

Since the early-1990s, the various definitions of new intermediate class have reflected the social fluidity and cultural distinctiveness of the employees of cognitive capitalism. Some neologisms can also be used as a description of the new ruling class: the Digital Citizen and the Bobos. Other definitions can also be applied to new working class: the Netizens, the Multipreneurs, the Digital Artisans, the New Independents, the Elancers, the Multitude, the Free Agents and the Pro-Ams. Most potent of all are those concepts which cover all three historic strands of the social prophecy: the Symbolic Analysts, the Virtual Class and the Creative Class. Avoiding the economic conflicts of the present, the promoters of these definitions emphasise the divide between those who cling to the past and those who are building the future. The Digital Citizens have more in common with the Digital Artisans than either of them do with their late-adopter class brethren who are off-line and out of touch. By excluding the providers of traditional – and essential – goods and services who make up the majority of the population, the differences between employers and employees within the hi-tech sectors can be made to disappear. Everyone within the creative industries is part of the futurist elite. Making new things in new ways with new technologies is the only prerequisite for membership of the class of the new.

Under Fordism, prominent theorists had defined this intermediate group by very different criteria. In the early-1970s, Nicos Poulantzas had characterised the New Petty-Bourgeoisie as the employees of the managerial hierarchy. Even office secretaries and bank clerks weren't worthy of inclusion within the heroic ranks of the exploited proletariat.[30] Although an extreme case, Poulantzas' suspicion of white-collar workers was shared by many on the Left. As the manual labourers below them knew all too well, these salaried bureaucrats were order-givers as well as order-takers. Just as importantly, as Poulantzas kept reminding his readers, many members of the New Petty-Bourgeoisie aped the conservative politics and mores of their superiors. Twenty years earlier, William Whyte had berated the Organisation Man not only for his 'cheerful acceptance of the *status quo*', but also for his 'disinterest in the arts.'[31] The path to a successful career within the Educational and Scientific Estate was internalising the routines and procedures of the corporate monolith. In its Fordist form, the educated conformist was epitome of the new intermediate class.

---

[30] See Nicos Poulantzas, *Classes in Contemporary Capitalism*, pages 211-212, 268-269.
[31] William Whyte, *The Organisation Man*, page 183.

The Class of the New

According to the 1990s gurus of the information economy, the attitudes of the Organisation Man were exactly what were not required. Controlling the workplace with a top-down bureaucracy was not only too expensive, but also, more importantly, too inflexible. Employees were now expected to manage themselves and set their own priorities. Released from the disciplines of Fordism, the Symbolic Analysts organised their own exploitation, the Multipreneurs ran their work lives as small businesses and the Free Agents were their own bosses. Above all, the members of the Creative Class had to be creative. Instead of repeating routines and following procedures, intellectuals, artists and techies were supposed to move beyond the curve and think outside of the box. Innovation not conformity was now the path to promotion. Aestheticism not philistinism had become the leitmotif of the new intermediate class. On her company's website, Helen Wilkinson praised the virtues of these pioneers of the dotcom future: '[the] Elancers are change agents, challenging traditional ways of working with their unique energy and spirit.'[32]

In his canonical text, Florida divided the class of the new into two distinct groups: the new ruling class and the new intermediate class. At the top of the social hierarchy were the visionaries of the Super-Creative Core who are responsible for 'the highest order of creative work': developing hardware, building software, making films, writing books, designing buildings and composing music. But, as Florida admitted, these innovators were only a small minority of the class of the new. Instead, the overwhelming majority of this group consisted of creative professionals '... who work in a wide range of knowledge-intensive industries such as high-tech sectors, financial services, the legal and healthcare professions, and business management.'[33] According to Florida, the continual expansion of the information economy was recruiting more and more people into the ranks of this intermediate layer. Because the boundaries of his new class were drawn so widely, he was convinced that - in the early-2000s - its members already made up as much as a third of the American workforce. Above all, Florida believed that the Super-Creative Core and the creative professionals were together pro-

---

[32] Elancentric, 'Project Description'.
[33] Richard Florida, *The Rise of the Creative Class*, page 69.

ducing half of the nation's wealth.[34] The descendents of the Bohemians had become the producers of economic abundance.

In the 2002 GLA report, the Mayor's statisticians were equally enthusiastic about the importance of London's Creative Class. According to the official figures for the late-1990s, the media, cultural and computing sectors had grown much faster than the rest of the local economy. After the sellers of business services, the creative industries had been the largest source of new jobs for Londoners in this period. By 2000, around 10% of the city's inhabitants were earning their living as artists, designers, programmers, technicians, writers, musicians, architects, actors, directors, copywriters and tailors – or by providing support for these professions.[35] Extrapolating from this evidence, the GLA report concluded that the expansion of the Creative Class would accelerate over the next few decades. Like Florida, its authors believed that they had identified the all important group which was prefiguring the future of the whole of society. In the post-Fordist economy, people increasingly expect goods and services that are tailored to their own needs and tastes. Whatever their line of business, if they wanted to meet this demand by making short-runs of specialised products, companies would have to imitate the flattened hierarchies and cooperative ethos of media, cultural and computing firms. Above all, they would also have to employ highly educated and self-motivated workers. In the epoch of cognitive capitalism, the Creative Class was the trailblazer for the entire city's economy.[36]

At the beginning of the GLA report, its authors reluctantly admitted that '... using official statistics is problematic.'[37] Crucially, the British government's employment surveys lumped together people with very different jobs under the same category because they happened to be working in the same industry. When they were on the payroll of a film company, security guards were transformed into members of the Creative Class. Yet, far from compensating for this inaccuracy, the authors of the GLA report engaged in their own inflation of the employment figures. When they were selling artworks and antiques, old-fashioned shopkeep-

---

[34] See Richard Florida, *The Rise of the Creative Class*, page xiv.
[35] See GLA Economics, *Creativity*, pages 4-11, 55-56.
[36] See GLA Economics, *Creativity*, page 6.
[37] GLA Economics, *Creativity*, page 3.

The Class of the New

ers were counted as part of the new class. This statistical massaging found its theoretical justification in Florida's book. Under his schema, the definition of the Creative Class covered almost all of the professions which didn't involve heavy manual labour or menial services. The new elite was open to everyone with taste, learning and imagination.

By exaggerating the size of the Creative Class, the Mayor's statisticians had tried to counter the sceptics who doubted that capitalism was undergoing another evolutionary mutation. Not surprisingly, in the aftermath of the dotcom bubble, the credibility of the McLuhanist prophecies of the digital utopia had been badly dented. If, even at the boom's peak, there had been more lorry drivers than computer programmers employed in the American economy, the rise of the Creative Class might be nothing more than another piece of Net hype.[38] Ironically, like the GLA report, this dissenting analysis was also fixated on the numbers game. The size of the Virtual Class was the measure of its economic importance. Depending upon how the figures were calculated, both boosters and critics could produce statistics which confirmed their own political positions.

In his introduction to the GLA report, Ken Livingstone welcomed the ascendancy of the Knowledge Workers as the harbinger of the next stage of modernity. However sophisticated, quantitative measures could never grasp the qualitative potential of this social group. Back in the mid-nineteenth century, the factory proletariat had also been only a minority of the English working class. The overwhelming majority of wage-earners were employed as unskilled labourers, shop assistants and household servants.[39] Yet, within a hundred years, the whole of society had been remodelled in the image of the Fordist factory. Market competition had systematically redistributed wealth from the labour-intensive to the capital-intensive branches of the economy.[40] Small businesses had fused into massive corporations. Politics had been rationalised. Everyday life had been

---

[38] See Doug Henwood, *After the New Economy*, pages 71-78, 184-185; and Aufheben, 'Keep on Smiling'.

[39] See Raphael Samuel, 'The Workshop of the World'.

[40] See Karl Marx, *Capital Volume 3*, pages 241-313.

The Makers of the Future

taken over by consumer culture.[41] In their definitions of the new class, thinkers of both the Right and the Left had anticipated this evolutionary path of capitalism. The Philosophers invented the machinery which was transforming the economy. The Labour Movement was forcing companies to adopt more sophisticated methods of production. The Bureaucrats and the Scientific Managers were building the political and economic hierarchies which would supplant liberalism. The Vanguard Party and the Samurai were precursors of the conspiratorial elite which would control these centralised power structures. Long before the triumph of Fordism, the theorists of the new class had described in detail the peculiarities of this particular stage of capitalist civilisation. The shape of the future could be discerned by analysing the makers of the future.

In the 1950s and 1960s, the high point of the bureaucratisation of society inspired a plethora of definitions: the Power Elite, the Organisation Man, Djilas' New Class, the Specialists, Galbraith's New Class, the Industrial Managers, the Order-Givers and the Technocrats. Yet, in the 1940s, Schumpeter's concept of the Entrepreneurs had already foreseen the transcendence of Fordism. By the time that this economic prophecy was fulfilled, thinkers from across the political spectrum had abandoned the bureaucratic archetype of the new class. Instead, their definitions emphasised the autonomy and independence of the youthful makers of the post-Fordist future. On the Right, the gurus of neo-liberal globalisation celebrated the ascendancy of the Gilder-style Entrepreneurs, the Venture Capitalists and the Symbolic Analysts. On the Left, the sages of community activism eulogised the emergence of the Hippies, the Produsumers, the Socialised Workers, the Nomads and the Post-Industrial Proletarians. Despite their deep political differences, all of these theorists were in agreement that capitalism was undergoing a fundamental transformation. Defining the new class was the most effective method of describing the emerging economic paradigm.

During the late-1990s dotcom boom, this post-Fordist vision of entrepreneurial employers and self-managing employees was promoted

---

[41] See Michel Aglietta, *A Theory of Capitalist Regulation*, pages 151-272; Alain Lipietz, *Towards a New Economic Order*, pages 1-13; and Henri Lefebvre, *Everyday Life in the Modern World*, pages 68-109.

The Class of the New

as the up-to-date business strategy of the information age. But, as Ken Livingstone pointed out in his introduction to the GLA report, management consultants have determinedly resisted this path of economic development for over two decades. McKinsey's experts argued that – instead of undermining corporate hierarchies – the convergence of the media, telecommunications and computing technologies was strengthening the power of the order-givers over the order-takers.[42] When production was outsourced to small businesses, the Post-Industrial Proletarians weren't liberated from the disciplines of the factory. On the contrary, thanks to the 'information Panopticon', the Scientific Managers were now able to monitor, audit and control the Knowledge Workers in much greater detail than the Fordist Workers had been subjected to in the past.[43] Best of all, by blocking the emergence of the self-directing Cognitariat, the McKinsey consultants could force the majority of the hi-tech labour force into the ranks of the exploited Precariat. The authoritarian definitions of the new class from the Fordist stage of capitalism had been updated and successfully imposed upon its post-Fordist iteration. Big was still beautiful in the age of the Net. But, when the dotcom bubble burst, the credibility of this analysis was undermined. One of the crash's most prominent casualties was the McKinsey consultancy's star pupil: Enron. Instead of building the hi-tech future, the tightening of top-down management had led to a litany of corporate failures: out-of-control executives, irrational investments, dodgy accounting and, finally, catastrophic bankruptcy.[44] Within the network economy, making new things with new technologies apparently implied new ways of working.

In contrast with the McKinsey experts, the neo-liberal proponents of the Digerati, the Digital Citizen, the Swarm Capitalists and the Bobos did realise that the hierarchies of Fordism weren't eternal. The centralisation of corporate and financial power at a global level – paradoxically – required the loosening of managerial controls within the most advanced sectors of production. Although confused by its technologi-

---

[42] For the McKinsey credo, see Tom Peters and Robert Waterman, *In Search of Excellence*.
[43] See Shoshana Zuboff, *In the Age of the Smart Machine*, pages 315-361.
[44] For an account of the rise and fall of Enron, see Bethany McLean and Peter Elkind, *The Smartest Guys in the Room*.

cal determinist assumptions, the McLuhanist prophecy had alerted the dotcom gurus to the economic consequences of the convergence of the media, telecommunications and computing. For the thinkers of the Right, their definitions of the new class explained how cutting-edge businesses were able to profit from this transformation. Similarly, for their rivals on the Left, concepts such as the Cyborgs, the Digital Artisans, the Immaterial Labourers, the Multitude, the Cognitariat, the Cybertariat and the Precariat described both the upsides and downsides of the knowledge economy for its workers. Whatever their political starting-point, these contemporary theorists of the new class have tried to anticipate the future of all of society by identifying its most developed sections in the present. They are convinced that – like the factory in earlier times – the network is more than just an economic phenomenon. All aspects of society are in the process of being restructured in its image.[45] More than any other group, the new class is at the forefront of the transition to cognitive capitalism. What they are doing today, everyone else will be doing tomorrow.

Over the past two centuries, successive definitions of the new class have provided inspiration for policy-makers. Since their predecessors had successfully predicted the advent of Fordism, the modern proponents of this social prophecy have an aura of credibility when they describe the advent of the knowledge economy. Following their path towards the future must be the route to success. Not surprisingly, the London Development Agency (LDA) – the GLA's economic arm – has prioritised its strategy for supporting the creative industries. As in other branches of production, the local state can help employers and employees in this sector by providing business advice, cheap premises, financial aid and educational opportunities.[46] In addition, the LDA set up an initiative to meet the specific needs of the knowledge economy: Creative London. Above all, its officials have had to develop policies which are suitable for the new conditions of cognitive capitalism. Back in the Fordist epoch, big business and big government were the two dominant methods of organising collective labour. But, as the contemporary definitions of the new class emphasise, these top-down structures are inca-

---

[45] See Benjamin Coriat, *L'Atelier et le Robot*, pages 25-31.
[46] See Creative London, *Believe*.

The Class of the New

pable of realising the full potential of the network economy. Responding to this new paradigm, the LDA has decided to foster the development of 'clusters' of creative firms. By congregating in particular areas of the city, the Swarm Capitalists are able to cooperate as well as compete with each other. By hanging out in these urban villages, the Cybertariat can help each other to find new jobs, learn new skills and discover new ideas.[47] Alongside the traditional duo of the market and the factory, the network has become the third – and most modern – method for organising collective labour.

As the LDA has realised, London has all the necessary ingredients for construction of thriving creative clusters. From medieval times onwards, particular trades have been associated with specific areas of the city. As the capital of the dominant imperial power of early modernity, London is home to the most ethnically diverse population on the planet. Since the 1950s, its youth subcultures have been renowned across the world. In the LDA's strategy, the creative cluster is the meeting place for these three sources of innovation. Brought together in a specific locality, the multi-ethnic and culturally sophisticated inhabitants of London are able to discover how to combine their individual talents for their mutual benefit. Like silk-weavers and cabinet-makers in the early-nineteenth century, the Digerati and the Digital Artisans of the 1990s were concentrated in Shoreditch. Speaking 300 different languages, the city's New Independents and Free Agents are its 'greatest competitive asset' in the global media marketplace.[48] Just like their youthful mod, punk and raver predecessors, the grown-up members of the Netocracy and the Cognitariat can be identified by their distinctive fashions and tastes in music. By fostering creative clusters, Ken Livingstone's administration – as the elected representative of the Labour Movement – is fulfilling its historical mission: accelerating the evolution of capitalism.

The origins of this economic development strategy can be traced back to the early-1980s. Two decades ago, Livingstone first became a national figure as the charismatic leader of the forerunner of the GLA: the Greater London Council (GLC). For five years, his administration's reforming programme was demonised in the media and frustrated by the

---

[47] See GLA Economics, *Creativity*, pages 31-50; and Creative London, *Believe*.
[48] GLA Economics, *Creativity*, page 33.

Thatcher government. When the GLC was eventually abolished in 1986, this progressive experiment appeared to have failed. But, by the time that Livingstone was elected Mayor of London in 2000, almost all of its radical ideas had become common sense: improving public transport; celebrating ethnic diversity; defending gay rights; making peace in Ireland and tackling police racism. However, these retrospective victories couldn't compensate for the GLC's economic defeat. During the first half of the 1980s, Livingstone's administration had tried - and failed - to halt the de-industrialisation of the local economy. Under the Thatcher government, finance and property were confirmed as the masters of London.[49] Twenty years ago, the GLC was a pioneer of economic policies which were specifically focused upon the creative industries. As well as encouraging cultural pluralism, these initiatives were also designed to increase employment opportunities and foster technological innovation. Although it was an important part of their overall strategy, the GLC's planners never believed that aiding this sector was a replacement for helping more traditional industries.[50] Two decades later, a different approach was needed. By the 2000s, the process of de-industrialisation in London had advanced much further. While other European counties are still major manufacturers, Britain has long forgotten that it was once the 'workshop of the world'. London's prosperity now depends upon its role as a global financial centre.

Like their GLC predecessors, the LDA's planners are also committed to reversing the decline of manufacturing. Even after two decades of neo-liberalism, this traditional sector is still an important provider of jobs. But, with financial institutions now dominating the local economy, providing support for the creative industries has become a higher priority. Both directly and indirectly, these businesses have benefited from the neo-liberal restructuring of London over the past twenty years. As the profits have flowed in from abroad, the financial sector has redistributed some of its wealth to the owners of advertising agencies, art galleries, entertainment venues and a host of other cultural enterprises. By 'pump-priming' these ventures, the 'trickle-down' of this money has underpinned two decades of growth in London's creative industries.

---

[49] For the story of the GLC, see Ken Livingstone, *If Voting Changed Anything, They'd Abolish It*; and Maureen Mackintosh and Hilary Wainwright, *A Taste of Power*.
[50] See GLC, *The London Industrial Strategy*; *The State of the Art or the Art of the State?*

The Class of the New

According to Florida, this phenomenon has wider economic benefits. From his research, he has concluded that cities like London with a thriving music scene and a large gay population are now the prime locations for hi-tech businesses. Even if they never go clubbing or are completely straight, members of the Creative Class want to live in hip and tolerant communities. Where the Digital Artisans congregate, the Swarm Capitalists who want to employ them must follow.[51] For the enlightened planners of the LDA, Florida's analysis gives political succour. Fostering creative clusters will not only create more jobs within this specific sector, but also could potentially reverse the decline of manufacturing in London. The prime location for software firms will attract hardware companies as well. When Silicon Valley was the icon of computerised modernity, its combination of lucrative military contracts and enthusiastic venture capitalists was almost impossible to replicate in a European setting. But, with Florida now anointing Austin as the prototype of the future, London has in abundance his prerequisites for becoming a flourishing digital city: bohemian ambience and cultural tolerance. All the LDA has to do is build upon what is already there.

Underneath its feel-good rhetoric, Florida's book also contains a more troubling message for the Mayor's planners: creative clusters are fragile structures. From the American experience, this theorist has concluded that gentrification doesn't just have negative consequences for the original inhabitants of inner-city areas.[52] If unchecked, this phenomenon will also seriously damage the local economy. Property speculators destroy the street life and community feeling which attract hi-tech firms to these locations in the first place. Rather than helping businesses, building shopping malls, yuppie flats and sports stadiums lowers a city's growth rate.[53] In London, the redevelopment of the East

---

[51] See Richard Florida, *The Rise of the Creative Class*, pages 235-260, 283-302.

[52] For an account of a local community's struggle against social cleansing in East London, see Hari Kunzru, 'A Dispatch from Tony's Café'. Anthony Iles and Ben Seymour's article, 'The (Re)Occupation', stresses that the Broadway Market campaign was primarily a battle to reinstate long-standing amenities of use to the (still) predominantly working class population of the area. For more info see: <34broadwaymarket.omweb.org>.

[53] See Richard Florida, *The Rise of the Creative Class*, pages 302-314.

End for the 2012 Olympics could be a repeat of this mistake. The disappearance of local retailers, low-cost housing, trendy clubs and art galleries would weaken rather than benefit the local economy. In the late-1990s, rising property prices led to an exodus of media and advertising companies from Soho to more hospitable boroughs.[54] As East London now also succumbs to the corporate monoculture, its vibrant creative cluster is similarly being broken up and dispersed across the city.[55] The financial institutions are not only a friend, but also an enemy of the new class. Their hunger for short-term speculative profits is a constant threat to the spatial and cultural foundations of London's long-term prosperity.

In a concluding flourish, Florida ended his book with a call to arms: the Creative Class must acquire 'class consciousness'. As the dominant group of the knowledge economy, its members have the awesome responsibility of leading the whole of society into the networked future.[56] By stressing this common purpose, Florida downplayed the divide between employers and employees within the Creative Class. The LDA's cluster strategy makes exactly the same assumption. The growth of the creative industries can deliver not only increasing profits, but also more jobs and rising wages. As the definitions of the Swarm Capitalists and the Multipreneurs have highlighted, it is becoming increasing difficult to distinguish the small business owners from the self-employed workers in this sector. In the defence of their hip neighbourhoods, the Bobos and the Multitude are united against the predations of property speculators and management consultants. These makers of the future – sometimes – do have consciousness of their common identity as the class of the new.

As part of its Creative London initiative, the LDA offers a free copyright advice service that: 'clues you up on how to protect and market your ideas.'[57] Like other aspects of the cluster strategy, the legal framework of intellectual property is assumed to be in the interest of both employers and employees. Over the last few decades, national govern-

---

[54] See Gautam Malkani, 'Look Beyond the Media Heartlands for the Full Story'.
[55] See Benedict Seymour, 'Shoreditch and the Creative Destruction of the Inner City'.
[56] See Richard Florida, *The Rise of the Creative Class*, pages 315-326.
[57] See Creative London, *Believe*, page 9.

ments and international agencies have been systematically tightening the copyright laws in response to lobbying from the creative industries. As with other commodities, information will only be produced if it can be sold for a profit in the marketplace. By copying intellectual property without payment, piracy disrupts the smooth functioning of the knowledge economy. In 2004, Estelle Morris – the British Arts Minister – declared that: 'Intellectual Property Rights have always been at the heart of our Creative Industries – by encouraging and rewarding creativity.'[58] According to the Blair government, the strict enforcement of the copyright laws was essential for transforming information into a commodity. If intellectual property wasn't protected, leading British companies would go bankrupt and large numbers of workers would lose their jobs. Copyright is the legal foundation for the economic well-being of all sections of the Creative Class.

During the late-1990s, neo-liberal politicians and pundits championed the Net as the pioneer of the global information marketplace. As shown by Amazon, e-Bay and other e-commerce sites, this new means of communications is an excellent tool for selling material goods and services. Ironically, what has been much more problematic is making money out of the iconic commodity of the neo-liberal knowledge economy: information. For over a decade, the music industry has been struggling to prevent people swapping tunes for free over the Net. Napster was closed down. Teenagers were taken to court. iTunes made it easy to pay for downloads. Yet, despite all these initiatives, a generation has grown up who think that paying for music is a choice not the rule. As connection speeds have increased, other creative industries are also having to face the same problem. If you know where to look, you can download your movies, software and games for free. Instead of providing the overarching legal structure for the information economy, the restrictions of copyright are only observed in the more legitimate areas of the Net. Even with advice from the LDA, London's creative cluster can't rely on the law to protect its ideas.

The prophets of neo-liberal McLuhanism were betrayed by their own favourite technology: the Net. In their visions of the imaginary

---

[58] Estelle Morris in Department of Culture, Media and Sports, 'Creative Industries Forum On Intellectual Property Launched'.

future, computer-mediated-communications was primarily a tool for buying and selling information commodities. Unfortunately for them, the Net was invented for a very different purpose: scientific research. Instead of organising their collective labour by trading information, academics work together by sharing knowledge with each other. Scientists advance up the career ladder by presenting papers at conferences, contributing articles to journals and distributing their findings for peer review. Not surprisingly, the pioneers of the Net built its architecture in their own image. By the time that business discovered the wonders of this technology, the social and cultural mores of the academic gift economy had been hardwired into its infrastructure. The Net is primarily a tool for sharing knowledge not selling information.[59] Repeatedly over the past decade, experts have confidently asserted that the days of the hi-tech gift economy are over. But, at each moment when big business appeared to have triumphed, the next iteration of cultural collectivism has swept across the network society: home made websites, virtual communities, open source software, P2P systems, blogging and locative media. In the late-2000s, the information Panopticon is an anachronism. Ubiquitous copyright isn't only unenforceable, but also undesirable.[60]

Within the academy, the scope of intellectual property is strictly limited. The peer review of scientific findings is founded upon sharing information. The critical analysis of different theories and empirical research depends upon the 'fair use' of material from copyrighted publications. This book itself is an example of how the academic gift economy advances understanding. Constructing a montage of quotations is a potent technique for telling the history of the theorists of the new class. Selecting particular passages – and leaving out others – imposes a specific theoretical interpretation on this collection of definitions. When included in this book, a thinker's analysis could be serving a very different purpose from that which was intended. Within the academic gift economy, knowledge must be shared not only among close colleagues, but also with bitter rivals. Under the rubric of 'fair use', the readers of this book are also encouraged to appropriate this

---

[59] See Richard Barbrook, 'The Hi-Tech Gift Economy'; and Mark Geise, 'From ARPAnet to the Internet'.

[60] See Richard Barbrook, 'The Regulation of Liberty'.

text for their own ends. This section can be cited and criticised. The quotations can be quoted. A different interpretation can be drawn from the same material. When downloaded in its digital form from the OpenMute website, this book can be easily sampled, reassembled and combined with other texts. In the information age, every reader can be an author.

This democratisation of creativity exposes a growing rift inside the Creative Class. In Florida's book, the same broad definition covered all three variants of the social prophecy: the new ruling class, the new intermediate class and the new working class. In its generosity, this concept encompassed both employers and employees. Despite the two sides of industry having some common interests, their attitudes towards copyright highlighted the differences between them. At the beginning of the dotcom boom, Netscape based its business strategy upon a paradoxical insight: software was 'free, but not free'.[61] Although this corporation is long gone, the creative industries are still coming to terms with this economic conundrum. For the Digerati who own intellectual property, the hi-tech gift economy is clearly a threat to their wealth and position. But, for the Immaterial Labourers, the position is much more ambiguous. On the one hand, the Multipreneurs want to be able to sell their work to others. On the other hand, the Cognitariat know how to get their software, music and films for free. When most members of the Creative Class don't respect the copyright laws, prosecuting teenagers for swapping tunes seems absurd. As Gilberto Gil – the Brazilian Minister of Culture and tropicalismo superstar – has urged, a rethink of the concept of intellectual property is now long overdue.[62] The smart Swarm Capitalists can find ways of making money within a post-Fordist paradigm where the boundaries between commodities and gifts are fuzzy: 'Those who obey the logic of the net … will have a keen advantage in the new economy.'[63]

For many on the Left, the withering away of intellectual property is a symbol of hope in pessimistic times. While most sectors of the economy are suffering from the tyranny of management consultants,

---

[61] For the story of Netscape, see Michael Cusumano and David Yoffie, *Competing on Internet Time*.

[62] See the interview with Gil in Julian Dibbell, 'We Pledge Allegiance to the Penguin'.

[63] Kevin Kelly, *New Rules for the New Economy*, page 160.

the creative industries are pioneering more participatory and fulfilling ways of working. During the past two decades, prominent thinkers on the Left have identified the employees of the knowledge economy as the new working class: the Cyborgs, the Digital Artisans, the Immaterial Labourers, the Multitude, the Cognitariat and the Cybertariat. Ironically, even these radical celebrations of post-Fordism are still caught up in the hierarchies of Fordism. As in the dotcom definitions of the Right, creativity is still a privilege of the few. Within the division of labour, a minority can make their living in this way only because the overwhelming majority of the population are doing other things. It was under Fordism that the separation of conception and action was pushed the furthest. The top-down rule of the Scientific Managers over the factory and the office rewarded obedience and punished initiative. Yet, even at the high point of this authoritarian system, the creativity of the Fordist Workers couldn't be completely suppressed. If they weren't allowed to express themselves at work, they seized the opportunities offered in their leisure time. The boredom of the assembly-lines was requited in the pleasures of hobbies.[64]

As the GLA report recognised, Londoners from all walks of life have helped to transform the city over the past fifty years from a drab imperial capital into a thriving creative centre. Ever since the 1950s, the trendsetters of its youth subcultures have played a key role in shaping its image as a cool and happening place. As both discerning consumers and innovative producers, they have defined the new styles in music, fashion, arts and design which London's creative industries have then successively sold to their admirers across the world. What has made these movements so attractive over the years to people from very different cultures and backgrounds is their celebration of self-expression. Frustrated at work, creativity reappears on the dance floor and in the streets. Being a clubber or a fashionista is much more exciting – and glamorous – than being a labourer or a bureaucrat. London's subcultures have always been much more than consumer cults. All of them have started as participatory movements. The new thing emerges within the community before it's repackaged as a commodity. In particular, this Do-It-Yourself attitude has shaped

---

[64] For an analysis of the differences between these two forms of working, see Miklós Haraszti, *Worker in a Worker's State*, pages 138-146.

The Class of the New

the city's music scene. London is a home of DJ culture: bootlegs, versions, remixes and mash-ups. Confounding the copyright purists, there are plenty of Londoners who don't just listen to music, but also make music with music. For a few, their extra-curricular activities can become a lucrative career, but, in most cases, making music remains a hobby. Long before the Net escaped from the universities, the bedroom DJs were working within a hi-tech gift economy.

Looking at London's recent cultural history, the limitations of Florida's thesis are exposed. Ironically, this theorist draws the boundaries of the Creative Class not only too widely, but also too narrowly. On the one hand, he includes people doing routine tasks which require little or no imagination within this sector. On the other hand, this theorist ignores the extent to which contemporary culture is a participatory phenomenon. Creativity isn't a monopoly of the Creative Class. The majority of the population who earn their living outside this sector can also be cultural producers. When Florida praises cities with hip music scenes, he misses that some of the coolest people in their clubs and bars aren't members of his new class. For them, creativity is what happens when they're playing outside work. In the past decade, the social impact of this DIY culture has been amplified by the spread of the Net. Amateurs are still responsible for the overwhelming majority of its content. In the mid-2000s, the most celebrated on-line businesses – like Flickr and MySpace – are services for self-publishing and community networking. The knowledge economy isn't just a new phase of capitalism, but also an evolutionary stage beyond capitalism. Alongside orders and commodities, gifts are now one of the principle methods of organising collective labour.[65] Back in the nineteenth century, some perceptive radicals anticipated this path of modernity in their concepts of the new class: the Bohemians, the General Intellect, the Educated Working Man and the Aristocracy of the Working Class. Since the 1960s, this vision of mass creativity has re-emerged as an influential archetype of the social prophecy: the Hippies, the Produsumers, the Prosumers, the Hackers, the Netizens, the Multitude and the Pro-Ams. In the infor-

---

[65] For an ironic take on this historical moment, see Richard Barbrook, 'Cyber-Communism'.

The Makers of the Future

mation society, making information is no longer solely the economic activity of a few professionals. As Joseph Beuys emphasised: 'The whole idea of creativity is a question of everyone's individual identity, a question of the identity of everyone on the Earth.'[66]

In this vision of mass participation, the prerequisite for the democratisation of culture is the breaking down of the division between mental labour and manual labour. For over two centuries, specialisation has been the path to prosperity. From Adam Smith onwards, thinkers in successive generations have identified the new class as the small group whose profession was inventing the future. As in other areas of the economy, experts were required to carry out this vital task efficiently. The few not the many were the builders of what was to come. In this book, the montage of quotations tracks the history of the different incarnations of this class of the new. In the late-nineteenth and early-twentieth centuries, the dominant archetypes of this social prophecy – more or less successfully – anticipated the evolutionary path of capitalism from liberalism into Fordism. During the past four decades, the theory of the new class has become identified with the advent of the knowledge economy. Like the factory in earlier times, the network will provide the model for the restructuring of the whole of society. But, as this collection of quotations demonstrates, the concept of the new class has never been a dispassionate method for analysing the human condition. On the contrary, the proponents of this social prophecy have always had a political agenda. Just like the predictions of technological determinists, their prophecies of the future were primarily prescriptions for the present. Knowing what will happen is a claim to control what is happening.

In the early-twenty-first century, identifying the class of the new has lost none of its political potency. On both the Right and the Left, thinkers are still promoting their ideological programmes in the guise of sociological analyses. Living in a country where cultural conformity is increasingly obligatory, Florida's definition of the Creative Class provides a convincing business rationale for opposing homophobia, racism and puritanism. Conservative Kansas is the Fordist past.[67] Bohemian Austin

---

[66] Joseph Beuys in Lucrezia de Domizio Durini, *The Felt Hat*, page 67.

[67] For a description of this antithesis of the creative city, see Thomas Frank, *What's The Matter With Kansas?*.

is the networked future. For the Mayor of London, the thesis of the Creative Class is also welcome. The hegemony of the management consultants – the ideologues of his political opponents inside and outside of the Labour party – will soon be over. The LDA's Creative London initiative is not only economically beneficial, but also politically rewarding. But, as Benjamin reminded his readers, the critical understanding of the present begins with the analysis of the past. For evaluating visions of the new class, this methodology is particularly essential. These prophecies of the future always look forward not backwards. However, like most influential concepts, this theory has a past. Florida's optimistic thesis of the Creative Class is a remix of an old tune. For a critical understanding of this social prophecy, examining its long history is essential. Because its nineteenth century proponents did foresee the rise of Fordism, does this necessarily mean that their twenty-first century successors' prophecies about cognitive capitalism are also correct? Above all, even if we agree with this prognosis, the question of *which* version of this post-Fordist paradigm will prevail is still open.

During the past thirty years, thinkers have repeatedly promoted their iterations of the Knowledge Class as the makers of the future. Compared to McKinsey's authoritarian credo, the neo-liberal Right's versions of this prophecy can appear progressive. This theory explains why property speculation and cultural authoritarianism are not only socially regressive, but also economically harmful. But, even in the Left's definitions, the elitism inherent in the Adam Smith's first iteration of the new class hasn't disappeared. However leftfield and wacky, the Cyborgs, the Digital Artisans, the Immaterial Labourers, the Multitude, the Cognitariat and the Cybertariat are still a privileged minority. If it wants to live up to its name, the LDA's Creative London initiative must be committed to supporting the mass creativity of all Londoners. Political democracy requires cultural democracy. If everyone is a voter, then everyone is also a creator. When mapping out the route to the future of libertarian social democracy, the vision of the new class must become inclusive. When everyone can participate within the General Intellect, creativity will no longer be a privilege. The class of the new will then be superseded by the civilisation of humanity.

4.
The Classes of the New

The Philosophers – Adam Smith (1776)

'Many improvements [in machinery] have been made by the ingenuity of ... those who are called philosophers or men of speculation, whose trade it is not to do any thing, but to observe every thing; and who, upon that account, are often capable of combining together the powers of the most distant and dissimilar objects. In the progress of society, philosophy or speculation becomes, like every other employment, the principal or sole trade and occupation of a particular class of citizens. Like every other employment too, it is subdivided into a great number of different branches, each of which affords occupation to a peculiar tribe or class of philosophers; and this subdivision of employment in philosophy, as well as in every other business, improves dexterity, and saves time. Each individual becomes more expert in his own peculiar branch, more work is done upon the whole, and the quantity of science is considerably increased by it.'

Adam Smith, *An Inquiry into the Nature and Causes of the Wealth of Nations*, page 14.

The Industrials – Henri Saint-Simon (1819)
'The national [industrial] party consists of:
Those whose work is of direct use to society.
Those who direct this work or whose capital is invested in industrial enterprises.
Those who contribute to production through work which is useful to the producers.'

> Henri Saint-Simon, 'Comparison Between the National (Industrial) Party and the Anti-National Party', page 187.

'Let us suppose that all of a sudden France loses fifty each of its best physicists, chemists, physiologists, mathematicians, poets, painters, sculptors, musicians, authors, mechanics, civil and military engineers, artillerymen, architects, doctors, surgeons, pharmacists, sailors, clockmakers, bankers; its two hundred best merchants and six hundred best farmers; fifty each of its best iron-masters, arms manufacturers, tanners, dyers, miners, manufacturers of cloth, cotton, silk, linen, ironmongery, earthenware and porcelain, crystal-[ware] and glassware; shipowners, carriers, printers, engravers, goldsmiths, and other metalworkers; masons, carpenters, joiners, blacksmiths, locksmiths, cutlers, foundrymen, and one hundred other persons in other unspecified posts, eminent in the sciences, fine arts, and arts and crafts, making in all the best scientists, artists, and artisans in France.*

As these Frenchmen are the most essential producers, those who provide the most important products, who direct the work which is most useful to the nation, and who are responsible for its productivity in the sciences, fine arts, and arts and crafts, they are really the flower of French society. Of all Frenchmen they are the most useful to their country, bringing it the most glory and doing most to promote civilisation and prosperity. The nation would become a lifeless corpse as soon as it lost them.

*Usually the term 'artisan' is only used to refer to ordinary workmen. In order to avoid circumlocution, we shall take this expression to mean everyone involved in material production, i.e. farmers, manufacturers, merchants, bankers, and all the clerks and workmen employed by them.'

> Henri Saint-Simon, 'A Political Parable', page 194.

The Civil Servants – Georg Hegel (1821)
'The universal class [of civil servants] has for its task the universal interests of the community.'

Georg Hegel, *The Philosophy of Right*, page 132.

'The maintenance of the state's universal interest, and of legality, in ... [the economic] sphere of particular rights, and the work of bringing these [self-interested] rights back to the universal, require to be superintended by ... (a) the executive civil servants, and (b) the higher advisory officials (who are organised in committees). These converge in their supreme heads who are in direct contact with the monarch.'

Georg Hegel, *The Philosophy of Right*, page 189.

'Between an individual [civil servant] and his office there is no immediate natural link. Hence individuals are not appointed to office on account of their birth or native personal gifts. The *objective* factor in their appointment is knowledge and proof of ability. Such proof guarantees that the state will get what it requires; and since it is the sole condition of appointment, it also guarantees to every citizen the chance of joining the class of civil servants.'

Georg Hegel, *The Philosophy of Right*, page 190.

'Civil servants and the members of the executive constitute the greater part of the middle class, the class in which the consciousness of right and the developed intelligence of the mass of the people is found.'

Georg Hegel, *The Philosophy of Right*, page 193.

The Bohemians – Adolphe d'Ennery and Grangé (1843)
'By "bohemians", I mean that class of individuals for whom existence is a problem, circumstances a myth, and fortune an enigma; who have no sort of fixed abode, no place of refuge; who belong nowhere and are met with everywhere; who have no particular calling in life but follow fifty professions; who, for the most part, arise in the morning without

knowing where they are to dine in the evening; who are rich today, impoverished tomorrow; who are ready to live honestly if they can, and otherwise if they cannot.'

Adolphe d'Ennery and Grangé, 'Les Bohémiens de Paris'.

The Bourgeoisie – Karl Marx and Friedrich Engels (1848)
'The bourgeoisie cannot exist without constantly revolutionising the instruments of production, and thereby the relations of production, and with them the whole relations of society. ... Constant revolutionising of production, uninterrupted disturbance of all social conditions, everlasting uncertainty and agitation distinguish the bourgeois epoch from all earlier ones. ... All that is solid melts into air ...'

Karl Marx and Friedrich Engels, *The Communist Manifesto*, page 17.

'The bourgeoisie ... has created more massive and colossal productive forces than have all preceding generations together. Subjection of Nature's forces to man, machinery, application of chemistry to industry and agriculture, steam-navigation, railways, electric telegraphs, clearing of whole continents for cultivation, canalisation of rivers, whole populations conjured out of the ground – what earlier century had even a presentiment that such productive forces slumbered in the lap of social labour?'

Karl Marx and Friedrich Engels, *The Communist Manifesto*, page 20.

The General Intellect – Karl Marx (1857)
'To the degree that ... direct labour and its quantity disappear as the determinant principle of production – of the creation of use values – and is reduced both quantitatively ... and qualitatively ... compared to general scientific labour, technological application of natural sciences, on one side, and to the general productive force arising from social combination in total production on the other side ... Capital thus works towards its own dissolution dominating production.'

Karl Marx, *Grundrisse*, page 700.

'Nature builds no machines, no locomotives, railways, electric telegraphs, self-acting mules etc. ... They are *organs of the human brain, created by human hand*; the power of knowledge, objectified. The development of fixed capital indicates to what degree general social knowledge has become a *direct force of production*, and to what degree, hence, the conditions of the process of social life itself have come under the control of the general intellect and have been transformed in accordance with it.'

Karl Marx, *Grundrisse*, page 706.

The Self-Made Man – Samuel Smiles (1859)

'It is the diligent head and hand alone that maketh rich – in self-culture, growth in wisdom, and in business. Even when men are born to wealth and high social position, any solid reputation which they may individually achieve can only be attained by energetic application; for though an inheritance of acres may be bequeathed, an inheritance of knowledge and wisdom cannot. ... Indeed, so far from poverty being a misfortune, it may, by vigorous self-help, be converted even into a blessing; rousing a man to that struggle with the world in which ... the right-minded and true-hearted find strength, confidence, and triumph.'

Samuel Smiles, *Self-Help*, pages 11-12.

The Labour Movement – Karl Marx (1867)

'... in the history of capitalist production, the establishment of a norm for the working day presents itself as ... a struggle between collective capital, i.e. the class of capitalists, and collective labour, i.e. the working class.'

Karl Marx, *Capital Volume 1*, page 344.

'[The] ... highly detailed specifications [of the Factory Acts], which regulate, with military uniformity, the times, the limits and the pauses of work by the stroke of the clock, were by no means a product of the fantasy of Members of Parliament. ... Their formulation, official recognition and proclamation by the state were the result of a long class struggle.'

Karl Marx, *Capital Volume 1*, pages 394-395.

'Factory legislation, that first conscious and methodical reaction of society against the spontaneously developed form of its production process, is ... just as much the necessary product of large-scale industry as cotton yarn, self-actors and the electric telegraph.'

Karl Marx, *Capital Volume 1*, page 610.

'If the general extension of factory legislation to all trades for the purpose of protecting the working class both in mind and body has become inevitable, ... that extension [also] hastens on the general conversion of numerous isolated small industries into a few combined industries carried on upon a large scale; it therefore accelerates the concentration of capital and the exclusive predominance of the factory system. ... While in each individual workshop it enforces uniformity, regularity, order and economy, the result of this immense impetus given to the technical improvement by the limitation and regulation of the working day is to increase the anarchy and the proneness to catastrophe of capitalist production as a whole, the intensity of labour, and the competition of machinery with the worker. ... By maturing the material conditions and the social combinations of the process of production, it matures the contradictions and antagonisms of the capitalist form of that process, and thereby ripens both the elements for forming a new society and the forces tending towards the overthrow of the old one.'

Karl Marx, *Capital Volume 1*, page 635.

The Educated Working Man – Thomas Wright (1868)

'The educated working man is the stock intelligent artisan improved and tempered by education. ... [He] ... is a well-read, well-informed member of society who has kept pace and is keeping pace with the progress of the age; a man who, having class interests, is yet capable of taking a broad and tolerant view of questions affecting those interests, and of clearly expressing and giving reasons for his own sentiments upon such questions; a man who can find his greatest gratification in intellectual pursuits and pleasures, and in his daily life displays in some greater or lesser degree that refinement which education gives.'

Thomas Wright, *The Great Unwashed*, pages 7-8.

The Superman – Friedrich Nietzsche (1883)

'You solitaries of today, you who have seceded from society, you shall one day be a people: from you, who have chosen out yourselves, shall a chosen people spring – and from this chosen people, the Superman.'

Friedrich Nietzsche, *Thus Spoke Zarathustra*, page 103.

'Artists, if they are any good, are (physically as well) strong, full of surplus energy, powerful animals, sensual; without a certain overheating of the sexual system a Raphael is unthinkable.'

Friedrich Nietzsche, *The Will to Power*, page 421.

'... as the consumption of ... mankind becomes more and more economical and the "machinery" of interests and services is integrated ever more intricately, a counter-movement is inevitable. ... [This will be] the production of a synthetic, summarising, justifying man for whose existence this transformation of mankind into a machine is a precondition, as a base on which he can invent his *higher form of being*.

He needs the opposition of the masses, of the "levelled", a feeling of distance from them! he stands on them, he lives off them. This higher form of aristocracy is that of the future.'

Friedrich Nietzsche, *The Will to Power*, pages 463-464.

The Aristocracy of the Working Class – Friedrich Engels (1885)

'... the great Trades' Unions ... are the organisations of those trades in which the labour of *grown-up men* predominates, or is alone applicable. Here the competition neither of women and children nor of machinery has so far weakened their organised strength. The engineers, the carpenters and joiners, the bricklayers, are each of them a power, to that extent that, as in the case of the bricklayers and bricklayers' labourers, they can even successfully resist the introduction of machinery. That their condition has remarkably improved since 1848 there can be no doubt, and the best proof of this is in the fact that for more than fifteen years not only have their employers been with them, but they with their employers, upon exceedingly good terms. They form an aristocracy among the working class; they have succeeded in enforcing for themselves a relatively comfortable position, and they accept it as final. They are the model working-men of Messrs. Leone Levi & Giffen, and they are very nice people indeed nowadays to deal with, for any sensible capitalist in particular and for the whole capitalist class in general.'

Friedrich Engels, *The Condition of the Working Class in England*, page 368.

The New Middle Class – William Morris (1885)

'I should like our friend to understand whither the whole system of palliation [through the Factory Acts] tends – namely, toward the creation of a new middle class to act as a buffer between the proletariat and their direct and obvious masters; the only hope of the bourgeoisie for retarding the advance of Socialism lies in this device. Let our friend think of a society thus held together. Let him consider how sheepishly the well-to-do workers today offer themselves to the shearer; and are we to help our masters to keep on creating fresh and fresh flocks of such sheep? What a society that would be, the main support of which would be capitalists masquerading as working men!'

William Morris, 'Socialism and Politics (An Answer to 'Another View')', pages 99-100.

The Intellectual Proletariat – William Morris (1888)
'The lower ranks of art and literature are crowded with persons drawn to these professions by the pleasantness of these pursuits in themselves, who soon find out the very low market value of the ordinary educated intellect. These, together with the commercial clerks, in whose occupation no special talent is required, form an intellectual proletariat whose labour is "rewarded" on about the same scale as the lower portion of manual labour, as long as they are employed, but whose position is more precarious, and far less satisfactory.'

>William Morris, 'Socialism From the Root Up', page 603.

The Vanguard Party – V.I. Lenin (1902)
'The active and widespread participation of the masses [in anti-monarchical politics] will ... benefit by the fact that a "dozen" experienced revolutionaries, trained professionally no less than the police, will centralise all the secret aspects of the work – drawing up leaflets, working out approximate plans and appointing bodies of leaders for each urban district, each factory and for each educational institution, etc. ...'

>V.I. Lenin, *What Is To Be Done?*, pages 154-155.

'It is ... our duty to assist every capable worker to become a *professional* agitator, organiser, propagandist, literature distributor, etc. etc. ... A worker agitator who is at all talented and "promising" *must not be left* to work eleven hours a day in a factory. We must arrange that he be maintained by the Party, that he may go underground at any time, that he change the place of his activity ... When we have detachments of specially trained worker-revolutionaries who have gone through extensive preparation ... no political police in the world will then be able to contend against them, for these detachments of men absolutely devoted to the revolution will themselves enjoy the absolute confidence of the masses of the workers.'

>V.I. Lenin, *What Is To Be Done?*, pages 162-164.

The Samurai – H.G. Wells (1905)

'Typically, the *samurai* are engaged in administrative work. Practically the whole of the responsible rule of the world is in their hands; all our head teachers and disciplinary heads of colleges, our judges, barristers, employers of labour beyond a certain limit, practising medical men, legislators, must be *samurai*, and all the executive committees ... that play so large a part in our affairs are drawn by lot exclusively from them. The order is not hereditary ... The *samurai* are, in fact, volunteers ... our Founders ... made a noble and privileged order ... open to the whole world.'

H.G. Wells, *A Modern Utopia*, pages 222-223.

The Bureaucrats – Max Weber (1910)

'Office holding is a 'vocation'. This is shown ... in the requirement of a firmly prescribed course of training ... and in the ... special examinations which are prerequisites of employment. Furthermore, the position of an official is in the nature of a duty. ... Entrance into an office [job], including one in the private economy, is considered an acceptance of a specific obligation of faithful management in return for a secure existence. ... Modern loyalty is devoted to impersonal and functional purposes.
...
Whether he is in a private office or a public bureau, the modern official always strives and usually enjoys a distinct *social esteem* as compared with the governed. His social position is guaranteed by the prescriptive rules of rank order ...'

Max Weber, *Essays in Sociology*, pages 198-199.

The Scientific Managers – Frederick Winslow Taylor (1911)

'[No] ... one workmen [has] the authority to make other men cooperate with him to do faster work. It is only through *enforced* standardisation of methods, *enforced* adoption of the best implements and working conditions, and *enforced* cooperation that this faster work can be assured. And the duty of enforcing the adoption of standards and of enforcing this cooperation rests with the *management* alone. The *management* must supply continually one or more teachers to show each new man the new and simpler motions, and the slower men must be constantly watched and helped until they have risen to their proper speed. All of those who, after proper teaching, either will not or cannot work in accordance with the new methods and at the higher speed must be discharged ... The *management* must also recognise the broad fact that workmen will not submit to this more rigid standardisation and will not work extra hard, unless they receive extra pay for doing it.'

Frederick Winslow Taylor, *The Principles of Scientific Management*, page 83.

The Labour Aristocracy – V.I. Lenin (1916)

'The upper layers [of the British working class] furnish the main body of co-operators, of trade unionists, of members of sporting bodies, and of numerous religious sects. ... Imperialism has ... a tendency to create privileged sections amongst the workers ... and to detach them from the main proletarian masses ... to encourage opportunism amongst them, and to give rise to a temporary organic decay in the working class movement ...'

V.I. Lenin, *Imperialism*, pages 124-125.

The Labour Bureaucracy – Gregory Zinoviev (1916)

'The great, overwhelming majority of the [labour movement's] functionaries are *workers*. ... But the concept "worker", in and of itself, must be applied with the greatest of care in this case. It would be better perhaps not to say "worker", but "worker in his origin." ... In reality, ... these people are no longer workers and have not been for decades. They have incomes bigger than the average bourgeois and have long ago given up their trades. ... They are workers in name only. In reality they are bureaucrats with a standard of living quite distinct from the average worker.

The worker-functionaries very often hail from the circles of the labour aristocracy. The labour *bureaucracy* and the labour *aristocracy* are blood brothers. The group interests of the one and the other very often coincide. Nevertheless, labour bureaucracy and labour aristocracy are two different categories.'

Gregory Zinoviev, 'The Social Roots of Opportunism', page 108

The Blackshirts – Mario Piazzesi (1921)
'For some time ... a new Italy has been forming, an Italy born of professionals, petty bourgeois artisans, peasants, common people, of all those who fought in the ... [First World War] ... It feels that the spirit of Victory is an idea which can nourish even simple souls.

New classes are forming who are leap-frogging the political and economic generations of before the war, most of them belonging to the small and middling bourgeoisie and artisan class. These have held military rank and have no intention of being absorbed back into the anonymous masses, but want to create new types of business, new companies, new trades in which to project the sense of leadership and organisation they learnt and applied in the war.'

Mario Piazzesi, 'The *Squadristi* as the Revolutionaries of the New Italy', page 39.

The Engineers – Thorstein Veblen (1921)
'In the beginning ... of the Industrial Revolution, there was no marked division between the industrial experts and the business managers. ... But from an early point in the development [of capitalism] there set in a progressive differentiation, such as to divide those who designed and administered the industrial processes from those others who designed and managed the commercial transactions and took care of the financial end. ...

This division between business management and industrial management has continued to go forward, at a continually accelerating rate, because the special training and experience required for any passably efficient organisation and direction of these industrial processes has continually grown more exacting, calling for specialised knowledge and abilities on the part of those who have this work to do and requiring their undivided interest and their undivided attention to the work at hand. But these specialists in technological knowledge, abilities, interest, and experience ... - inventors, designers, chemists, mineralogists, soil experts, crop specialists, production managers and engineers of many kinds and denominations – have continued to be employees of ... the captains of finance, whose work it has been to commercialise the knowledge and abilities of the industrial experts and turn them to account for their own gain.'

Thorstein Veblen, *The Engineers and the Price System*, pages 76-77.

'These expert men, technologists, engineers ... make up the indispensable General Staff of the industrial system; and without their immediate and unremitting guidance and correction the industrial system would not work. It is a mechanically organised structure of technical processes designed, installed, and conducted by these production engineers. Without them and their constant attention the industrial equipment, the mechanical appliances of industry, will foot up to just so much junk.'

Thorstein Veblen, *The Engineers and the Price System*, pages 82-83.

The Fordist Worker – Henry Ford (1922)

'I am now most interested in fully demonstrating that the ideas we have put into practice [at the Ford Motor Company] are capable of the largest application – that they have nothing peculiarly to do with motor cars ... but form something in the nature of a universal code.'

Henry Ford, *My Life and Work*, page 3.

'The net result of the application of ... [the] principles [of the assembly-line] is the reduction of the necessity for thought on the part of the worker and the reduction of his movements to a minimum. He does as nearly as possible only one thing with only one movement.'

Henry Ford, *My Life and Work*, page 80.

'... to the majority of minds, repetitive operations hold no terrors. In fact, to some types of mind ... the ideal job is one where the creative instinct need not be expressed. ... The average worker ... wants a job in which he does not have to put forth much physical exertion – above all, he wants a job in which he does not have to think.'

Henry Ford, *My Life and Work*, page 103.

'[Our policy of raising wages] ... was a sort of prosperity-sharing plan. But on conditions. The man and his home had to come up to certain standards of cleanliness and citizenship. ... the idea was that there should be a very definite incentive to [morally] better living and that the very best incentive as a money premium on proper living. A man who is living alright will do his work alright.'

Henry Ford, *My Life and Work*, page 128.

The Open Conspiracy – H.G. Wells (1928)

'... when we come to the general functioning classes, landowners, industrial organisers, bankers and so forth, who control the present system ... it is very largely from the ranks of these classes and from their stores of experience and traditions of method, that the directive forces of the new order must emerge. ... There are no doubt many ... [who act] for personal or group advantage to the general detriment. ... But there remains a residuum of original and intelligent people ... who are curious about their own intricate function and disposed towards a scientific investigation of its origins, conditions and future possibilities. Such types move naturally towards the Open Conspiracy. ...

Now the theme of the preceding paragraph might be repeated with ... appropriate modifications ... [for] the industrial organiser, the merchant and organiser of transport, the advertiser, the retail distributor, the agriculturalist, the engineer, the builder, the economic chemist, and a number of other types functional to the contemporary community. In all we should distinguish ... an active, progressive section to whom we should turn naturally for developments leading towards the progressive world commonweal of our desires.'

H.G. Wells, *The Open Conspiracy*, pages 57-58.

The Intellectuals – Antonio Gramsci (1934)

'School is the instrument through which intellectuals of various levels are elaborated. The complexity of the intellectual function in different states can be measured objectively by the number and gradation of specialised schools: the more extensive the "area" covered by education and the more numerous the "vertical" "levels" of schooling, the more complex is the cultural world, the civilisation, of a particular state.'

Antonio Gramsci, *Selections From the Prison Notebooks*, pages 10-11.

'The intellectuals are the dominant group's "deputies" exercising the subaltern functions of social hegemony and political government.'

Antonio Gramsci, *Selections From the Prison Notebooks*, page 12.

'Intellectuals of the urban type have grown up along with industry and are linked to its fortunes. ... Their job is to articulate the relationship between the entrepreneur and the [proletarian] instrumental mass and to carry out the immediate execution of the production plan decided by the industrial general staff, controlling the elementary stages of work. On the whole, the average urban intellectuals are very standardised, while the top intellectuals are more and more identified with the industrial general staff itself.'

Antonio Gramsci, *Selections From the Prison Notebooks*, page 14.

The Managerial Class – James Burnham (1941)

'We may often recognise them as 'production managers', operating executives, superintendents, administrative engineers, supervisory technicians; or, in government (for they are to be found in governmental enterprise just as in private enterprise) as administrators, commissioners, bureau heads, and so on. ... [The] managers ... [are] those who already ... are actually managing, on its technical side, the actual process of production, no matter what the legal and financial form – individual, corporate, governmental – of the process.'

James Burnham, *The Managerial Revolution*, page 81.

'The managers ... naturally tend to identify ... the salvation of mankind with their assuming control of society. Society can be run, they think, in more or less the same way that they know they ... can run, efficiently and productively, a mass-production factory.'

James Burnham, *The Managerial Revolution*, page 177.

The Entrepreneurs – Joseph Schumpeter (1942)
'[The] ... function of entrepreneurs is to reform or revolutionise the pattern of production by exploiting an invention or, more generally, an untried technological possibility for producing a new commodity or producing an old one in a new way, by opening up a new source of materials or a new outlet for products, by reorganising an industry and so on. ... To undertake such new things is difficult and constitutes a distinct economic function, first, because they lie outside of the routine tasks which everybody understands and, secondly, because the environment resists in many ways that vary, according to the social conditions, from simple refusal to finance or to buy a new thing, to physical attack on the man who tries to produce it. To act with confidence beyond the range of familiar beacons and to overcome that resistance requires aptitudes that are present in only a small fraction of the population and that define the entrepreneurial type as well as the entrepreneurial function. This function does not essentially consist in either inventing anything or otherwise creating the conditions which the enterprise exploits. It consists in getting things done.'

Joseph Schumpeter, *Capitalism, Socialism and Democracy*, page 132.

The Inner Party – George Orwell (1948)
'The new aristocracy was made up for the most part of bureaucrats, scientists, technicians, trade-union organisers, publicity experts, sociologists, teachers, journalists and professional politicians. These people, whose origins lay in the salaried middle class and the upper grades of the working class, had been shaped and brought together by the barren world of monopoly industry and centralised government. ...

Individually, no member of the Party owns anything, except petty personal belongings. Collectively, the Party owns everything ... because it controls everything, and disposes of the products as it thinks fit.'

George Orwell, *Nineteen Eighty-Four*, page 166.

The New Middle Class – C. Wright Mills (1951)
'... the white-collar workers ... are expert at dealing with people transiently and impersonally; they are masters of the commercial, professional and technical relationship. The one thing they do not do is live by making things; rather, they live off the social machineries that organise and coordinate the people who do make things. ... They are the people who keep track; they man the paper routines involved in distributing what is produced. They provide technical and personal services, and they teach others the skills which they themselves practice, as well as all other skills transmitted by teaching.'

C. Wright Mills, *White Collar*, pages 65-66

'The historic bases of the white-collar employees' prestige ... have included the similarity of their place and type of work to those of the old middle-classes ... Furthermore, the time taken to learn ... [their] skills and the way in which they have been acquired by formal education and by close contact with the higher-ups in charge has been important. ... White-collar employees are the assistants of authority; the power they exercise is a derived power, but they do exercise it.'

C. Wright Mills, *White Collar*, pages 73-74.

The Power Elite – C. Wright Mills (1956)
'There is no longer, on one hand, an economy, and, on the other hand, a political order containing a military establishment unimportant to politics and money-making. There is [instead] a political economy linked, in a thousand ways, with military institutions and decisions. ... As each of these domains has coincided with the

others, ... the leading men in each of the three domains of power – the warlords, the corporation chieftains, the political directorate – tend to come together, to form the power elite of America.'

C. Wright Mills, *The Power Elite*, pages 7-9.

'All those who succeed in America ... are likely to become involved in the world of celebrity. This world ... has been created from above. Based upon nation-wide hierarchies of power and wealth, it is expressed by nation-wide means of communications. ...

With the incorporation of the economy, the ascendancy of the military establishment, and the centralisation of the enlarged state, there have arisen the national elite, who, in occupying the command posts of the big hierarchies, have taken the spotlight of publicity and become the subjects of the intensive build-up. At the same time, with the elaboration of the national means of mass communications, the professional celebrities of the entertainment world have come fully and continuously into the national view.'

C. Wright Mills, *The Power Elite*, page 71.

The Organisation Man – William Whyte (1956)

'These people only work for The Organisation. They are the ... mind and soul of our great self-perpetuating institutions. ...

The corporation man is the most conspicuous example ... [of how] the collectivisation so visible in the corporation has affected almost every field of work. Blood brother to the business trainee off to join Du Pont is the seminary student who will end up in the church hierarchy, the doctor headed for the corporate clinic, the physics PhD in a government laboratory, the intellectual on the foundation-sponsored team project, the engineering graduate in the huge drafting room at Lockheed, the young apprentice in a Wall Street law factory.

... Listen to them talk to each other over the front lawns of their suburbia and you cannot help but be struck by how well they grasp the common denominators which bind them.'

William Whyte, *The Organisation Man*, page 8.

'Look at a cross section of [managers'] profiles and you will see three denominators shining through: extroversion, disinterest in the arts, and a cheerful acceptance of the *status quo*.'

William Whyte, *The Organisation Man*, page 183.

The New Class – Milovan Djilas (1957)
'The ownership principles of the new class and membership in that class are the privileges of *administration*. This privilege extends from state administration and the administration of economic enterprises to that of sports and humanitarian organisations. Political, party, or so-called "general leadership" is executed by the core [of the new class].'

Milovan Djilas, *The New Class*, page 54.

'Membership in the Communist [Vanguard] Party before the Revolution meant sacrifice. Being a professional revolutionary was one of its highest honours. Now that the party has consolidated its power, party membership means that one belongs to a privileged class. And at the core of the party are the all-powerful exploiters and masters.'

Milovan Djilas, *The New Class*, page 55.

The Specialists – Ralf Dahrendorf (1957)
'In the enterprises of post-capitalist society, ... [a] complex system of delegation of responsibility obliterates ... the dividing line between positions of domination and subjection. ... there are ... groups that stubbornly resist allocation to one or the other quasi-group. One of these consists of the "staff" of the enterprise, the engineers, the chemists, physicists, lawyers, psychologists, and other specialists whose services have become an indispensable part of production in modern firms. ... the class situation of specialists in the enterprise remains as uncertain as the class situation of intellectuals in society. They are neither superordinates nor subordi-

nates; their positions seem to stand beyond the authority structure. Only insofar as they can be identified as (often indirect) helpers of management, can they be called a marginal part of the ruling class of the enterprise.'

Ralf Dahrendorf, *Class and Class Conflict in an Industrial Society*, page 255.

The New Class – J.K. Galbraith (1958)

'The New Class is not exclusive. ... Any individual whose adolescent situation is such that sufficient time and money are invested in his preparation, and who has at least the talents to carry him through the formal academic routine, can be a member. ...

Some of the attractiveness of membership in the New Class ... derives from a vicarious feeling of superiority ... However, membership in the class unquestionably has other and more important rewards. Exemption from manual toil; escape from boredom and confining and severe routine; the chance to spend one's life in clean and physically comfortable surroundings; and some opportunity for applying one's thoughts to the day's work ...

This being so, there is every reason to conclude that the further and rapid expansion of this class should be ... *the* major social goal of the [affluent] society.'

John Kenneth Galbraith, *The Affluent Society*, pages 275-276.

The Industrial Managers – Clark Kerr (1960)

'Industrial managers, private or public, and their technical and professional associates ... are the "vanguard [party]" of the future. It is they who largely create and apply the new technology, who determine the transformations in skills and responsibilities, who influence the impact of such changes upon the work force and who exercise leadership in a technological society.'

Clark Kerr, John Dunlop, Frederick Harbison and Charles Myers, *Industrialism and Industrial Man*, page 30.

'Management ... includes entrepreneurs, managers, administrators, engineers and professional specialists who hold the top positions in an enterprise. In this hierarchy, the organisation builder plays a critical role. He may be the owner of the business, a professional private manager or a government official. He is the keystone in the arch of management ...'

Clark Kerr, John Dunlop, Frederick Harbison and Charles Myers, *Industrialism and Industrial Man*, page 134.

'There is ... no precise dividing line between the managerial group and the industrial labour force. ... In some cases foremen are members of the management; in others they are the highest ranking members of the labouring class. ... With this qualification, the working force may said to include the following: manual labour of all skill levels, [and] clerical workers ... whereas administrators, professional employees, engineers, and scientists are clearly in the managerial category.'

Clark Kerr, John Dunlop, Frederick Harbison and Charles Myers, *Industrialism and Industrial Man*, page 165.

The Order-Givers - Cornelius Castoriadis (1961)

'At the objective level, the transformation of capitalism is expressed in increasing bureaucratisation. The roots of this tendency are in production, but they extend and finally invade all sectors of social life. Concentration of capital and statification are but different aspects of the same phenomenon. ...

The inherent objective ... of bureaucratic capitalism is the construction of a totally hierarchical society in constant expansion, a sort of monstrous pyramid where the increasing alienation of men in labour will be "compensated" by a steady rise in the standard of living, all initiative remaining in the hands of the organisers. ... The increasing bureaucratisation of all social activities only succeeds in extending into all social domains the conflict inherent in the division of society into order-givers and order-takers. ... The inherent irrationality of capitalism remains but now finds expression in new and different ways.'

> Paul Cardan [Cornelius Castoriadis], *Modern Capitalism and Revolution*, page 3.

The New Working Class – Serge Mallet (1963)
'Workers employed in automated industries (or industries in the process of automation) have been called the "new working class". In fact, this term covers two different types of wage earners, both born of new technical developments and both involved in this process of "integration in the firms".

The new factory uses two types of workers who are still classified as manual workers. These are the foremen, loaders, operators, and preparers who are assigned to automated production units; and the maintenance workers, who are in charge of repairing and keeping watch over the machinery. ….

The other group, numerically greater, is not exclusively born of automation, but is partly due to the trend in modern industry to devote much time and effort to operations anterior to the classic production process (studies and research) and beyond it (commercialisation, market research, etc.). … The enormous development of research units has … created real intellectual production units, in which working conditions grow increasingly similar to those of a modern workshop, but devoid of physical strain, dirt and stink – though with the same planned timing and mechanisation of office work.'

> Serge Mallet, *The New Working Class*, pages 66-68.

The Knowledge Workers – Peter Drucker (1966)
'Modern society is a society of large organised institutions. In every one of them, including the armed services, the centre of gravity has shifted to the knowledge worker, the man who puts to work what he has between his ears rather than the brawn of his muscles or the skill of his hands.'

> Peter Drucker, *The Effective Executive*, page 3.

'The imposing system of measurements and tests which we have developed for manual work – from industrial engineering to quality control – is not applicable to knowledge work. ... Working on the *right* things is what makes knowledge work effective. This is not capable of being measured by any of the yardsticks for manual work.

The knowledge worker cannot be supervised closely or in detail. He can only be helped. But he must direct himself, and he must direct himself towards performance and contribution, that is effectiveness.'

Peter Drucker, *The Effective Executive*, pages 3-4.

'Knowledge work is not defined by quantity. Neither is knowledge work defined by its costs. Knowledge work is defined by its results. And for these, the size of the [administrative] group and the magnitude of the managerial job are not even symptoms.'

Peter Drucker, *The Effective Executive*, page 7.

The Educational and Scientific Estate – J.K. Galbraith (1967)

'As the trade unions [of the industrial working class] retreat ... into the shadows, a rapidly growing body of educators and research scientists emerges. This group connects at the edges with scientists and engineers within the [corporate] technostructure and with civil servants, journalists, writers and artists outside. Most directly nurtured by the industrial system are the educators and scientists in the schools, colleges, universities and research institutions. They stand in relation to the industrial system much as did the banking and financial community to the earlier stages of industrial development. ... Education ... has now the greatest solemnity of social purpose.'

The educational and scientific estate, like the financial community before it, acquires prestige from the productive agent that it supplies. Potentially, at least, this is also a source of power.'

John Kenneth Galbraith, *The New Industrial State*, pages 286-287.

The Class of the New

The Technocrats – Alain Touraine (1969)
'Technocrats are not technicians but managers, whether they belong to the administration of the State or to big businesses which are closely bound, by reason of their very importance, to the agencies of political decision-making.'

   Alain Touraine, *The Post-Industrial Society*, pages 49-50.

'If property was the criterion of membership of the former dominant classes, the new dominant class [of technocrats] is defined by knowledge and a certain level of education.'

   Alain Touraine, *The Post-Industrial Society*, page 51.

'The principal opposition between ... [the] two great classes ... does not result from the fact one possesses wealth and property and the other does not. It comes about because the dominant classes dispose of knowledge and control *information*.'

   Alain Touraine, *The Post-Industrial Society*, page 61.

'... today's programmed society ... [is] dominated by the new conflict between technocrats and consumers ...'

   Alain Touraine, *The Post-Industrial Society*, page 192.

The Hippies – Abbie Hoffman and Jerry Rubin (1969)
'It was a phenomenal burst of human energy and spirit that came and went like a tidal wave up there in ... Woodstock, Aquarian Exposition, Music Festival, Happening, Monster, or whatever you called the fuckin thing. I took a trip to our future. That's how I saw it. Functional anarchy, primitive tribalism, gathering of the tribes. Right on!'

   Abbie Hoffman, *Woodstock Nation*, page 13.

'Like almost everyone in the left, I have a genuine suspicion about the mass media, especially television. [However] ... some day real soon most families in [the American] PIG NATION will be able through their TV sets to have a computer at their disposal ... the most revolutionary means of communications since language itself was invented.'

Abbie Hoffman, *Woodstock Nation*, page 105.

'Our youth ghettos must have a communal economy so we can live with one another, trading and bartering what we need. A free community without money.

We will organise our own record companies, publishing houses and tourist companies so profit will come back into the community for free food, free rent, free medical care, free space, free dope, free living, community bail funds.

Thousands of us have moved from the cities into the country to create communes. Dig it! The communes will bring food into the city in exchange for services which the urban communes will bring to the country.'

Jerry Rubin, *Do It!*, page 236.

'The world will become one big commune with free food and housing, everything shared. All watches and clocks will be destroyed. ... There will be no such crime as "stealing" because everything will be free. The [US military's] Pentagon [headquarters] will be replaced by an LSD experimental farm. There will be no more schools or churches because the entire world will become one church and school. People will farm in the morning, make music in the afternoon and fuck wherever and whenever they want to.'

Jerry Rubin, *Do It!*, page 256.

The Produsumers – Décio Piganatari (1969)
'The collage is the provisional syntax of creative synthesis, a mass syntax. The collage is the assembly of simultaneity, a general totem. ... Technology is achieving such sophistication that it starts to require the year zero of a NEW BARBARISM to unblock its pores. Society is ever more rich, life is ever more poor. ... Today's models of con-

sumption are the models of production of 40 years ago ... This is the time of PRODUSUMERISM. The student is for the university what the worker is for the factory. The student is the information worker. Students in the [political and ideological] superstructure are still copying the old models of struggle of workers in the [economic] base. [This is the time of] PRODUSUMERISM. The world of consumption is superseded by the world of information, where the decisive battle will take place. NEW BARBARISM: an open field for the new models of the information war. The elites, especially the academic ones, are rotten with stupidity: every new [produsumer] barbarian knows more than them. It is not necessary to wait until everyone owns a motor car for the new culture to be born. Ownership is for the world of things, culture is for the world of signs. The artist is a language designer, even if – and especially if – they're marginalised. This is the [time of the] artistic guerilla. ... Collective joy is the final vindication: intimacy in deep harmony. Beyond the ciphers. And against the [tyranny of the] $$.'

Décio Pignatari, *Contracomunicacao*, page 27.

The Scientific Intellectual Labourers – Ernest Mandel (1972)

'Economically, the ... main characteristics of the third technological revolution [of nuclear energy, cybernetics and automation] can be discerned: A qualitative acceleration in ... the displacement of living by dead labour. ...

A shift of living labour power still engaged in the process of production from the actual treatment of raw materials to preparatory or supervisory functions. ... The scientists, laboratory workers, projectors and draughtsmen who work in the forecourt of the actual production process also perform ... surplus value-creating labour. ...'

Ernest Mandel, *Late Capitalism*, pages 194-195.

'The age of the third technological revolution is necessarily an epoch of [the] unprecedented fusion of science, technology and production. ... In increasingly automated production there is no further place for unskilled factory or office workers. A massive and generalised transformation of manual into intellectual work is not only made possible, but also economically and socially essential by automation.'

Ernest Mandel, *Late Capitalism*, page 215.

'The social position of all those social groups that occupationally participate in supervising the extraction of surplus-value from the commodity labour-power or the preservation of constant capital by labour-power, typically induces a general identification with the class interests of the entrepreneurial bourgeoisie. It might even be said that such identification is a precondition of the performance of their specific function ... [within the] factory or society. ... By contrast, intellectually qualified workers engaged in the immediate process of production or reproduction, or those whose social function does not necessarily come into collision with the class interest of wage-earners – for example, health-insurance doctors or social workers employed by a local authority – are ... more likely to align themselves with the ... proletariat.'

Ernest Mandel, *Late Capitalism*, page 265.

The Knowledge Class – Daniel Bell (1973)

'If the dominant figures of the past hundred years have been the entrepreneur, the businessman and the industrial executive, the "new men" are the scientists, the mathematicians, the economists and the engineers of the new intellectual technology. ...

In the post-industrial society, ... the crucial decisions regarding the growth of the economy and its balance will come from government, but they will be based on the government's sponsorship of research and development, of cost-effectiveness and cost-benefit analysis; the making of decisions ... will have an increasingly technical character. The husbanding of talent and the spread of educational and intellectual institutions will become a prime concern of society; not only the best talents but eventually the entire complex of prestige and status will be rooted in the intellectual and scientific communities.'

Daniel Bell, *The Coming of Post-Industrial Society*, pages 344-345.

'If one turns ... to the societal structure of the post-industrial society ... two conclusions are evident. First, the major class of the new society is primarily a professional class, based on knowledge rather than property. But second, the control system of the society is lodged not in a successor-occupational class but in the political order, and the question who manages the political order is an open one. ...

In terms of status (esteem and recognition, and possibly income), the knowledge class may be the highest class in the new society but in the nature of that structure there is no intrinsic reason for this class, on the basis of some coherent or corporate identity, to become a new economic interest class, or a new political class which would bid for power.'

Daniel Bell, *The Coming of Post-Industrial Society*, page 374-375.

The Intermediate Layers – Harry Braverman (1974)

'Among ... [the] intermediate groupings are parcelled out the specialised bits of knowledge and delegated authority without which the machinery of production, distribution and administration would cease to operate. ... Their conditions of employment are affected by the need of top management to have within its orbit buffer layers, responsive and "loyal" subordinates, transmission agents for the exercise of control and the collection of information, so that management does not confront unaided a hostile or indifferent [working class] mass. ... All in all, ... those in this area of capitalist employment enjoy, in greater or lesser degree depending upon their specific place in the hierarchy, the privileges of exemption from the worst features of the proletarian situation, including, as a rule, significantly higher scales of pay. ...

This "new middle class" ... occupies its intermediate position not because it is *outside* the process of increasing capital [as with the old middle class], but because, as part of this process, it takes its characteristics from *both sides*. Not only does it receive its petty share in the prerogatives and rewards of capital, but it also bears the mark of the proletarian condition.'

Harry Braverman, *Labour and Monopoly Capital*, pages 406-407.

The New Petty-Bourgeoisie – Nicos Poulantzas (1974)

'[The] ... engineers and technicians ... [of the new petty-bourgeoisie] are often themselves responsible for the work of management and supervision; they directly control the 'efficiency' of the workers and the achievement of output norms. ...

Their mental labour, separated from manual labour, represents the exercise of political relations in the despotism of the factory, legitimised by, and articulated to, the monopolisation and secrecy of knowledge, i.e. the reproduction of the ideological relations of domination and subordination.'

Nicos Poulantzas, *Classes in Contemporary Capitalism*, pages 239-240.

'The various [new] petty-bourgeois agents each possess, in relation to those subordinate to them, a fragment of the fantastic secret of knowledge that legitimises the delegated authority that they exercise. This is the very meaning of [bureaucratic] 'hierarchy'.'

Nicos Poulantzas, *Classes in Contemporary Capitalism*, page 275.

'[The] ... petty-bourgeois ideological sub-ensemble is a terrain of struggle and a particular battlefield between bourgeois ideology and working-class ideology, though with the specific intervention of peculiarly petty-bourgeois elements.'

Nicos Poulantzas, *Classes in Contemporary Capitalism*, page 289.

The Professional-Managerial Class – Barbara & John Ehrenreich (1975)

'We define the Professional-Managerial Class [PMC] as consisting of salaried mental workers who do not own the means of production and whose major function in the social division of labour may be described broadly as the reproduction of capitalist culture and capitalist class relations.

Their role in the process of reproduction may be more or less explicit, as with workers who are directly connected with social control or with the production and propagation of ideology (e.g. teachers, social workers, psychologists, entertainers, writers of advertising copy and TV scripts, etc.). Or it may be hidden within the process of production, as is the case with the middle-level administrators and managers, engineers, and other technical workers whose functions ... are essentially determined by the need to preserve the capitalist relations of production. Thus we assert that these occupational groups – cultural workers, managers, engineers and scientists, etc. – share a common function in the broad social division of labour and a common relation to the economic foundations of society.

The PMC ... includes people with a wide range of occupations, skills, income levels, power and prestige. The boundaries separating it from the ruling class above and the working class below are fuzzy. ... occupation is not the sole determinant of class (nor even the sole determinant of the relation to the means of production).'

Barbara & John Ehrenreich, 'The Professional-Managerial Class', pages 12-13.

The Proletarianised Professionals – Stanley Aronowitz (1975)

'As the logic of capital requires a more minute division of labour, more sophisticated integrative mechanisms, enlarged state intervention into the economy, and a larger army of administrative workers, the size of the middle strata of professionals grows. At the same time, those lacking power and authority within the administrative and state sectors also grow. The army of clerical workers, operators of duplicating, accounting, bookkeeping, and other machines accompanies the employment of computer professionals, accountants, designers, and other professionals.

Although clerical workers such as typists, secretaries and office machine operators are certainly part of the working class, their position is by no means unambiguous in the social structure. ... Head offices of large corporations and state bureaucracies are apparatuses of bourgeois ideological hegemony as well as social domination. The institutions of schools, health care, and administration ... function to reproduce capitalist social relations and culture, as well as facilitate the accumulation and reproduction of capital. ...

What is more, often the clerical functions overlap with those of technicians and professionals. The number of "managers" of clerical workers is extremely high in proportion to those who are designated as "clerical" employees. ... This tendency is particularly pronounced in the telephone and other branches of the communications industry where the proportion of supervisors to workers is about one to three. In addition, many of those designated in the job categories as technicians and professionals find that, as mechanisation replaces a large number of tasks that were previously skilled aspects of their professions, these college educated, professionally trained employees are reduced to clerical workers.'

Stanley Aronowitz, 'The Professional-Managerial Class or Middle Strata', page 236.

The Post-Modernists – Jean-François Lyotard (1979)

'It is widely accepted that knowledge has become the principle force of production over the last few decades; this has already had a noticeable effect on the composition of the work force of the most highly developed countries ... In the post-industrial and post-modern age, science will maintain and no doubt strengthen its pre-eminence in the arsenal of productive capacities of the nation-states.'

Jean-François Lyotard, *The Post-Modern Condition*, page 5.

'[The post-modern] ... orientation corresponds to the course that the evolution of social interaction is currently taking; the temporary contract is in practice supplanting permanent institutions in the professional, emotional, sexual, cultural, family, and international domains, as well as in political affairs. This evolution is of course ambiguous: the temporary contract is favoured by the system due to its greater flexibility, lower cost, and the creative turmoil of its accompanying motivations ... We should be happy that the tendency toward the temporary contract is ambiguous ...This bears witness to the existence of another goal with the system: knowledge of [multiple] language games as such and the decision to assume responsibility for their rules and effects. ...

We are ... in a position to understand how the computerisation of society affects this problematic. It could become the "dream" instrument for controlling and regulating the market system, extended to include knowledge itself and governed exclusively by the performativity principle. ... But it could also aid groups discussing metaprescriptives by supplying them with the information which they usually lack for making knowledgeable decisions. The line to follow for the second of these two paths is, in principle, quite simple: give the public free access to the [computer] memory and data banks.'

Jean-François Lyotard, *The Post-Modern Condition*, pages 66-67.

The Socialised Workers – Antonio Negri (1980)

'This [new] proletariat is fully social ... and it has extended the contradiction/antagonism against capitalist accumulation of profit from the factory area to the whole of society. It has been responsible for upsetting and destabilising the whole circuit from production to reproduction. And it has developed the contradiction of the social conditions of the reproduction of labour-power as an obstacle against capital accumulation. ... It has above all represented *a new quality of labour*. This ... represents a mobile sort of labour force, both horizontally and vertically, a labour-power which is abstract, and which projects new needs. ... For this ... proletariat, wage gains went hand in hand with advances in the social wage and the conquest of free time.'

Antonio Negri, 'The Crisis of the Crisis-State', page 183.

'... when the whole of life becomes production, capitalist time measures only that which it directly commands. And socialised labour-power tends to unloose itself from command, insofar as it proposes a life-alternative – and thus projects a different time for its own existence, both in the present and in the future. When all life-time becomes production-time, who measures whom? *The two conceptions of time and life* come into direct conflict in a separation which becomes increasingly deep and rigidly structured.'

Antonio Negri, 'Archaeology and Project', page 220.

'The ... [historical] process, concomitant with those of individual marginalisation and collective socialisation, has brought about a conjunction between (a) the refusal of labour-power to make itself available as a commodity (... the effect of individual marginalisation and the collapse of any relationship between "job" and "skill") and (b) the socialisation of this mode of class behaviour.'

Antonio Negri, 'Archaeology and Project', page 223.

The White-Collar Proletarians – Michael Kelly (1980)
'Market Situation.
Income proletarianisation ... the incomes of white-collar workers have fallen relatively or absolutely [compared] to those of manual workers ...
Different sources of income ... the incomes of non-manual workers are derived increasingly from their own productive labour and less from the productive labour of others ...
Feminisation ... the white-collar workforce is becoming increasingly feminine in character ...
Social origin ... the white-collar labour force is becoming increasingly "proletarian" in origin as children of manual workers move into non-manual occupations ...

Work Situation
Bureaucratisation ... as large-scale organisations become increasingly big, they become increasingly bureaucratic and the employee loses his identity as a specialist or professional ...
Mechanisation and automation ... with changes in the division of labour brought about by technological advances, the functions and nature of clerical work have changed, producing routinisation and repetitiveness ...

Michael Kelly, *White-Collar Proletarians*, page 23.

The Nomads – Gilles Deleuze and Félix Guattari (1980)
'The more the worldwide [capitalist] axiomatic installs high industry and highly industrialised agriculture at the periphery [of the world economy], provisionally reserving for the centre so-called post-indus-

trial activities (automation, electronics, information technologies, the conquest of space, overarmament, etc.), the more it installs peripheral zones of underdevelopment inside the centre, internal Third Worlds, internal Souths. "Masses" of the population are abandoned to erratic work (subcontracting, temporary work, or work in the underground economy), and their official subsistence is assured only by State allocations and wages subject to interruption. ... In enslavement and the central dominance of constant capital ... labour seems to have splintered into two directions: intensive surplus labour that no longer even takes the route of labour, and extensive labour that has become erratic and floating. ... The opposition between the [capitalist] axiomatic and the [nomadic] flows it does not succeed in mastering becomes all the more accentuated.'

Gilles Deleuze and Félix Guattari, *A Thousand Plateaus*, page 469.

'We can say of the nomads ... *they do not move*. They are nomads by dint of not moving, not migrating, of holding a smooth space that they refuse to leave ... To think is to voyage ... It is not a question of returning to ... the ancient nomads. The confrontation between the smooth [nomad space] and the striated [space of the State apparatus is] ... under way today, running in the most varied directions.'

Gilles Deleuze and Félix Guattari, *A Thousand Plateaus*, page 482.

The Prosumers – Alvin & Heidi Toffler (1980)

'Above all, ... Third Wave [post-industrial] civilisation begins to heal the historic breach between producer and consumer, giving rise to the "prosumer" economics of tomorrow. For this reason, among many, it could – with some intelligent help from us – turn out to be the first truly human civilisation in recorded history.'

Alvin Toffler, *The Third Wave*, pages 24-25.

'Many of the same electronic devices we will use in the home to do work for pay will also make it possible to produce goods or services for our own use. In this system, the prosumer, who dominated in First Wave [agricultural] societies, is brought back into the centre of economic action – but on a Third Wave [post-industrial], high-technology basis.'

Alvin Toffler, *The Third Wave*, page 286.

'Given home computers, given seeds genetically designed for urban or even apartment agriculture, given cheap home tools for working plastic, given new materials, adhesives, and membranes, and given free technical advice available over the telephone lines with instructions perhaps flickering on the TV or computer screen, it becomes possible to create lifestyles that are more rounded and varied, less monotonous, more creatively satisfying, and less market-intensive than those that typified Second Wave [industrial] civilisation.'

Alvin Toffler, *The Third Wave*, pages 289-290.

The Post-Industrial Proletarians – André Gorz (1980)

'This ... [social group] encompasses all those who have been expelled from production by the abolition of work, or whose capacities are under-employed as a result of the industrialisation (in this case, the automation and computerisation) of intellectual work.'

André Gorz, *Farewell to the Working Class*, page 68.

'[The] ... traditional working class is now no more than a privileged minority. The majority of the population now belongs to the post-industrial neo-proletariat which, with no job security or definite class identity, fills the area of probationary, contracted, casual, temporary and part-time employment. In the not too distant future, jobs such as these will be largely eliminated by automation. Even now, their ... requirements bear little relation to the knowledge and skills offered by schools and universities. The neo-proletariat is generally over-qualified for the jobs it finds.'

André Gorz, *Farewell to the Working Class*, page 69.

'Whether they work in a bank, the civil service, a cleaning agency or a factory, neo-proletarians are basically non-workers temporarily doing something that means nothing to them. They do "any old thing" which "anyone" can do, provisionally engaged in temporary and meaningless work.'

André Gorz, *Farewell to the Working Class*, pages 70-71.

The Entrepreneurs – George Gilder (1981)

'Entrepreneurial learning is of a deeper kind than is taught in schools, or acquired in the controlled experiments of social or physical science, or gained in the experience of socialist economies. For entrepreneurial experiments are also adventures, with the future livelihood of the investor at stake. He participates with a heightened consciousness and passion and an alertness and diligence that greatly enhance his experience of learning. The experiment may reach its highest possibilities, and its crises and surprises may be exploited to the utmost.'

George Gilder, *Wealth and Poverty*, page 35.

'Material progress is ineluctably elitist: it makes the rich richer and increases their number, exalting the few extraordinary men who can produce wealth over the democratic masses who consume it. Material progress depends upon the expansion of opportunity: geniuses identify themselves chiefly through their works rather by their inheritance or test scores. Material progress is difficult: it requires from its protagonists long years of diligence and sacrifice, devotion and risk that can be elicited only with high rewards, not the "average return on capital." ... Material progress is inimical to scientific economics: it cannot be explained or foreseen in mechanistic or mathematical terms.'

George Gilder, *Wealth and Poverty*, page 273.

'Some are scientists, some are artists, some are craftsmen; most are in business. ... They are not always kind or temperate, rarely elegant or tall, only occasionally glib or manifestly leaders of men. ... As immigrants, many deliberately seek an orphan's fate, and toil to launch a dynasty. ... Mostly outcasts, exiles, mother's boys, rejects, warriors, they learn early the lessons of life, the knowledge of pain, the ecstasy of struggle. ...

The so-called means of production are impotent to generate wealth and progress without the creative men of production, the entrepreneurs.'

George Gilder, *The Spirit of Enterprise*, pages 17-19.

'In business as in art, the individual vision prevails over the corporate leviathan; the small company ... confounds the industrial policy; the entrepreneur dominates the hierarch. The hubristic determinisms of the academy and the state – the secular monoliths of science and planning, the imperial sovereigns of force and finance – give way to one man working in the corner of a lab or a library.'

George Gilder, *The Spirit of Enterprise*, page 243.

The Venture Capitalists – John Naisbitt (1982)

'American entrepreneurship has gotten a big boost in recent years with the abrupt increase in venture-capital money. ... What was behind the impressive upsurge in venture capital? For one thing, small business can thank [US] government policy – in 1978, the capital-gains tax was reduced from 49 to 28 percent. That certainly helped. ...

But there are other reasons behind the new abundance in venture capital: More and more people are learning that entrepreneurship pays off. Sophisticated venture capitalists are willing to take a calculated risk in return for a possible 20 to 25 percent return. When stock market returns average below 10 percent and even money-market funds can barely keep pace with inflation, backing new businesses starts to look more attractive. ...

Furthermore, venture capitalists can now choose from a great number of more sophisticated, more experienced entrepreneurs who are better managers and whose ideas are well thought-out.

All totalled, entrepreneurial self-help is an idea whose time has come again, and the 1970s were its debut decade.'

John Naisbitt, *Megatrends*, pages 147-148.

The Hackers – Steven Levy (1984)

'[The] ... hackers – those computer programmers and designers who regard computing as the most important thing in the world – ... were adventurers, visionaries, risk-takers, artists ... and the ones who most clearly saw why the computer was truly a revolutionary tool. ... As I talked to these digital explorers ... I found a common element ... It was a philosophy of sharing, openness, decentralisation, and getting your hands on machines at all costs – to improve the machine, to improve the world. This Hacker Ethic is their gift to us: something with value even to those of us with no interest at all in computers.'

Steven Levy, *Hackers*, page 7.

'The people in [the] Homebrew [Computer Club] were a mélange of professionals too passionate to leave computing at their jobs, amateurs transfixed by the possibilities of technology, and techno-cultural guerrillas devoted to overthrowing an oppressive society in which government, business, and especially IBM had relegated computers to a despised Priesthood [of authorised users].'

Steven Levy, *Hackers*, page 205.

The Cyborgs – Donna Haraway (1985)

'The "New Industrial Revolution" is producing a new world-wide working class, as well as new sexualities and ethnicities. The extreme mobility of capital and the emerging international division of labour are intertwined with the emergence of new collectivities, and the weakening of familiar groupings. ... In the prototypical Silicon Valley, many women's lives have been structured around employment in electronics-dependent jobs, and their intimate realities include serial heterosexual monogamy, negotiating childcare, distance from extended kin or most other forms of traditional community, a high likelihood of loneliness and extreme economic vulnerability as they age. The ethnic and racial diversity of women in Silicon Valley structures a microcosm of conflicting differences in culture, family, religion, education, and language.'

Donna Haraway, 'A Cyborg Manifesto', page 166.

'"Networking" is both a feminist practice and a multinational corporate strategy – weaving is for oppositional cyborgs.'

Donna Haraway, 'A Cyborg Manifesto', page 170.

'Cyborg imagery ... is a dream not of a common language, but of a powerful infidel heteroglossia. It is an imagination of a feminist speaking in tongues to strike fear into the circuits of the super-savers of the new right. It means both building and destroying machines, identities, categories, relationships, space stories. Though both are bound in the spiral dance, I would rather be a cyborg than a goddess.'

Donna Haraway, 'A Cyborg Manifesto', page 181.

The Symbolic Analysts – Robert Reich (1991)

'Included in this category are the problem-solving, [problem]-identifying, and [strategic-]brokering of many people who call themselves research scientists, design engineers, software engineers, civil engineers, biotechnology engineers, sound engineers, public relations executives, investment bankers, lawyers, real estate developers, and even a few creative accountants. Also included is much of the work done by management consultants, financial consultants, tax consultants, energy consultants, agricultural consultants, armaments consultants, architectural consultants, management information specialists, organisation development specialists, strategic planners, corporate headhunters, and systems analysts. Also: advertising executives and marketing strategists, art directors, architects, cinematographers, film editors, production designers, publishers, writers and editors, journalists, musicians, television and film producers, and even university professors.

Symbolic analysts solve, identify, and broker problems by manipulating symbols. They simplify reality into abstract images that can be rearranged, juggled, experimented with, communicated to other specialists, and then, eventually, transformed back into reality. The manipulations are done with analytical tools, sharpened by experience. The tools may be mathematical algorithms, legal arguments, financial gimmicks, scientific principles, psychological insights about how to persuade or to amuse, systems of induction or deduction, or any other set of techniques for doing conceptual puzzles.'

>Robert Reich, *The Work of Nations*, pages 177-178.

The Virtual Class – Arthur Kroker and Michael Weinstein (1994)

'The economic base of the virtual class is the entire communications industry – everywhere it reaches. ... The most complete representative of the virtual class is the visionary capitalist who is constituted by all of its contradictions and who, therefore, secretes its ideological hype. The rest of the class tends to split the contradictions: the visionless-cynical-business capitalists and the perhaps visionary, perhaps skill-orientated, perhaps indifferent techno-intelligentsia of cognitive scientists, engineers, computer scientists, videogame developers, and all the other communication specialists, ranged in hierarchies, but all dependent for their economic support on the drive to virtualisation. Whatever contradictions there are within the virtual class – that is, the contradictions stemming from the confrontation of bourgeois and proletarian – the class as a whole supports the drive into cyberspace through the wired world.'

>Arthur Kroker and Michael Weinstein, *Data Trash*, page 15.

'The virtual class wants to appropriate emergent technologies for purposes of authoritarian political control over cyberspace. It wants to drag technotopia back to the age of the primitive politics of predatory capitalism.'

>Arthur Kroker and Michael Weinstein, *Data Trash*, page 16.

The Netizens – Michael & Ronda Hauben (1995)

'My research demonstrated that there were people active as members of the network, which the words net citizen did not precisely represent. The word citizen suggests a geographic or national definition of social membership. The word Netizen reflects the new non-geographically based social membership. ...

This definition is used to describe people who care about Usenet and the bigger Net and work towards building the [system's] cooperative and collective nature which benefits the larger world. ... As more and more people join the online community and contribute towards the nurturing of the Net and toward the development of a great shared social wealth, the ideas and values of Netizenship spread.'

Michael Hauben and Ronda Hauben, *Netizens*, pages x-xi.

The Digerati - John Brockman (1996)

'The "digerati" ... are *a* cyber elite ... they constitute a critical mass of doers, thinkers, and writers, connected in ways they may not even appreciate, who have a tremendous influence on the emerging communication revolution surrounding the growth of the Internet and the World Wide Web. Although they all happen to be American, their activities have a worldwide impact.'

John Brockman, *Digerati*, page xxxi.

'Many of the brightest people in recent years have gone into computing (hardware, networking, software, Internet, convergence media). The cutting edge is exploring new communications, such as the World Wide Web, through the use of computers ... the digerati ... (as well as others) ... are driving this revolution. ... This ... group of people ... are reinventing culture and civilisation.'

John Brockman, *Digerati*, page xxxii.

The Multipreneurs - Tom Gorman (1996)

'To become a multipreneur you must realise that your economic value depends upon your ability to make or save money for others and your ability to add value to processes. Your economic value will not depend upon your position, seniority or connections. You must therefore train yourself to see opportunities where others see problems, dislocations, and barriers. You must choose your assignments on the basis of the skills you can learn as well as those you can apply. You must develop your interpersonal and technological skills to a high level so that you can make things happen rather than hope they will happen.'

> Tom Gorman, *Multipreneuring*, pages 11-12.

'In multipreneuring you develop a portfolio of jobs, projects, businesses, and income streams as well as a portfolio of knowledge, skills, contacts, and credentials. Like an investor, you must actively manage your portfolio. This entails balancing risks and returns, desires and obligations, the future and the present. So your employment portfolio should include ... movement toward your deepest dreams as an artist, athlete or public servant or world traveller, as well as the work that pays the bills (may the two someday be one for you). It should include skill-[building], contact-[building], and knowledge-building activities for your next career move and the move after that, as well as activities that add high value to your current situation.'

> Tom Gorman, *Multipreneuring*, page 258.

The Immaterial Labourers – Maurizio Lazzarato (1996)

'All the characteristics of the post-industrial economy ... are heightened within the form of "immaterial" production properly defined: audiovisual production, advertising, fashion, the production of software, photography, cultural activities, etc.

The activities ... of immaterial labour ... are the result of a synthesis of various types of savoir-faire (those of intellectual activities, as regards the cultural-informational content; those of manual activities for the ability to put together creativity, imagination and technical and manual labour; and that of entrepreneurial activities for that capacity of management of their social relations and of structuration of the social cooperation of which they are a part).'

> Maurizio Lazzarato, 'General Intellect', page 2.

'It is immaterial labour which continually innovates the form and the conditions of communication (and thus of work and consumption). It gives form and materialises needs, images, the tastes of consumers and these products become in their turn powerful producers of needs, of images and of tastes.'

Maurizio Lazzarato, 'General Intellect', page 3.

'Waged labour and direct subjugation (to organisation) are no longer the principle form of the contractual relationship between capitalist and worker; polymorphous autonomous work emerges as the dominant form, a kind of "intellectual worker" who is himself an entrepreneur, inserted within a market that is mobile and within networks that are changeable in time and space.'

Maurizio Lazzarato, 'General Intellect', page 4.

The Digital Artisans – Richard Barbrook and Pit Schultz (1997)

'For those of us who want to be truly creative in hypermedia and computing, the only practical solution is to become digital artisans. The rapid spread of personal computing and now the Net are the technological expressions of this desire for autonomous work. Escaping from the petty controls of the shopfloor and the office, we can rediscover the individual independence enjoyed by craftspeople during proto-industrialism. ... We create virtual artifacts for money and for fun. We work both in the money-commodity economy and in the gift economy of the Net. When we take a contract, we are happy to earn enough to pay for our necessities and luxuries through our labours as digital artisans. At the same time, we also enjoy exercising our abilities for our own amusement and for the wider community. Whether working for money or for fun, we always take pride in our craft skills. We take pleasure in pushing the cultural and technical limits as far forward as possible. We are the pioneers of the modern.'

Richard Barbrook and Pit Schultz, 'The Digital Artisans Manifesto',
page 53.

The Digital Citizen – Jon Katz (1997)

'... there is indeed a distinct group of Digital Citizens. ... they're knowledgeable, tolerant, civic-minded, and radically committed to change. Profoundly optimistic about the future, they're convinced that technology is a force for good and that our free-market economy functions as a powerful engine of progress. ... they ... view our existing political system positively, even patriotically. ... The Internet ... encompasses many of the most informed and participatory citizens we have ever had or are likely to have. ... [The] profile of this rising group ... [is] based on ... [the people who] use email and ... have access to a laptop, a cell phone, a beeper and a home computer.'

Jon Katz, 'The Digital Citizen', page 71.

The Swarm Capitalists – Kevin Kelly (1998)

'The internet model has many lessons for the new economy but perhaps the most important is its embrace of dumb swarm power. The aim of swarm power is superior performance in a turbulent environment. When things happen fast and furious, they tend to route around central control. By interlinking many simple parts into a loose confederation, control devolves from the centre to the lowest or outermost points which collectively keep things on course.'

Kevin Kelly, *New Rules for the New Economy*, page 16.

'Numerous small things connected together into a network generate tremendous power. But this swarm power will need some kind of minimal governance from the top to maximise its usefulness. Appropriate oversight depends upon the network. In a firm, leadership is supervision; in social networks, government; in technical networks; standards and codes.'

Kevin Kelly, *New Rules for the New Economy*, page 18.

'The future of technology is networks. Networks large, wide, deep, and fast. Electrified networks of all types will cover our planet and their complex nodes will shape our economy and colour our lives. ... Those who obey the logic of the net, and who understand that we are entering into a realm with new rules, will have a keen advantage in the new economy.'

Kevin Kelly, *New Rules for the New Economy*, page 160.

The New Independents – Charlie Leadbeater and Kate Oakley (1999)

'The [New] Independents ... are a driving force of ... [economic] growth. A large and growing share of employment in ... [the creative] industries is accounted for by the self-employed, freelancers and micro-businesses. These new Independents are often producers, designers, retailers and promoters all at the same time. They do not fit into neat categories. The Independents thrive on informal networks through which they organize work, often employing friends and former classmates. Although some are ambitious entrepreneurs, many want their businesses to stay small because they want to retain their independence and their focus on their creativity. Yet that does not mean they see themselves as artists who deserve public subsidy. They want to make their own way in the market. They have few tangible assets other than a couple of computers. They usually work from home or from nondescript and often run-down workshops. Their main assets are their creativity, skill, ingenuity and imagination.'

Charlie Leadbeater and Kate Oakley, *The Independents*, page 11.

'*They blur the demarcation line between work and non-work.* As consumption and leisure are inputs into the creation of cultural products, the corollary is that periods not at work – leisure, relaxation, entertainment – can be as important as periods at work hunched over a computer terminal. Both contribute to delivering a creative product. Many of these independents say their best ideas come to them when they are not at work.'

Charlie Leadbeater and Kate Oakley, *The Independents*, page 24.

The Elancers – Helen Wilkinson (1999)

'More and more organisations are out-sourcing work, and are reliant on a new breed of flexible, independent workers, otherwise known as the elancer. Elancers lack the support structures of a typical head office environment and are reliant on the Internet to organize their work and communicate with colleagues. They tend to be self-employed, mobile consultants, freelancers, contractors, even remote workers for large organisations. ... Elancers are change agents, challenging traditional ways of working with their unique energy and spirit – something we call elancentricity. ... Join this exciting new community and help map the new terrain that is the elancescape.'

Elancentric, 'Project Description'.

The Multitude – Antonio Negri and Michael Hardt (2000)

'With the computerisation of production today ... the heterogeneity of concrete labour has tended to be reduced, and the worker is increasingly further removed from the object of his or her labour. The labour of computerised tailoring and the labour of computerised weaving may involve exactly the same concrete practices – that is, manipulation of symbols and information. ... The computer proposes itself ... as the universal tool ... through which all activities might pass. Through the computerisation of production, then, labour tends towards the position of abstract labour.'

Antonio Negri and Michael Hardt, *Empire*, page 292.

'Immaterial labour immediately involves social interaction and cooperation. In other words, the cooperative aspect of immaterial labour is not imposed or organised from the outside, as it was in previous forms of labour, but rather, *cooperation is completely immanent to the labouring activity itself*. ... Today productivity, wealth, and the creation of social surpluses take the form of cooperative interactivity through linguistic, communicational, and affective networks.'

Antonio Negri and Michael Hardt, *Empire*, page 294.

'The mode of production of the multitude reappropriates wealth from capital and also constructs new wealth, articulated with the powers of science and social knowledge through cooperation. .... Private property of the means of production today, in the era of the hegemony of cooperative and immaterial labour, is only a putrid and tyrannical obsolescence. The tools of production tend to be recomposed in collective subjectivity and in the collective intelligence and affect of the workers; entrepreneurship tends to be organised by the cooperation of subjects in [the] general intellect. ... The multitude is biopolitical self-organisation.'

Antonio Negri and Michael Hardt, *Empire*, pages 410-411.

The New Barbarians – Ian Angell (2000)

'Make way for the barbarians (old and new), the opportunists awaiting their chance to hijack the future, and form a new order. ... They are the press and media barons, the market manipulators, international businesspeople, international terrorists, 'downsized' states, criminal conspiracies, drugs barons, neo-colonialist non-governmental organisations, economic mercenaries, financial plutocrats, religious and political fundamentalists, amoral individualists: the new you and the new me? They are the power brokers, now cut free from the constraints of national boundaries by the new communication technologies. ... The barbarians know that their time is coming, for natural selection is on their side; history is on their side.'

Ian Angell, *The New Barbarian Manifesto*, page 26.

The Bobos (Bourgeois Bohemians) – David Brooks (2000)

'In this era, ideas and knowledge are at least as vital to economic success as natural resources and finance capital. ... So the people who thrive in this period are the ones who can turn ideas and emotions into products. These are highly educated folk who have one foot in the bohemian world of creativity and another foot in the bourgeois realm of ambition and worldly success. The members of the new information age elite are bourgeois bohemians. Or, to take the first two letters of each word, they are Bobos.'

David Brooks, *Bobos in Paradise*, pages 10-11.

'Work ... becomes a vocation, a calling, a metier. And the weird thing is that when employees start thinking like artists and activists, they actually work harder for the company. ... if work is a form of self-expression or a social mission, then you never want to stop. You are driven by a relentless urge to grow, to learn, to feel more alive.'

David Brooks, *Bobos in Paradise*, page 135.

'Bobo businesspeople have created a corporate style attuned to the information age, with its emphasis on creativity, flat hierarchies, flexibility and open expression. It's simply impossible to argue with the unparalleled success of America's information age industries over the past decade.'

David Brooks, *Bobos in Paradise*, page 269.

The Cognitariat – Franco Bifo Berardi (2001)

MF: In your new book, 'The Factory of Unhappiness' you describe a class formation, the 'cognitariat' – a conflation of cognitive worker and proletarian ... You've also previously used the idea of the 'Virtual Class'. What are the qualities of the cognitariat and how might they be distinguished from this slightly higher strata depicted by Kroker and Weinstein in *Data Trash*?

Bifo: I like to refer to the concept of virtual class, which is a class that does not actually exist. It is only the abstraction of the fractal ocean of productive micro-actions of the cognitive workers. It is a useful concept, but it does not comprehend the existence (social and bodily) of those people who perform virtual tasks. But the social existence of virtual workers is not virtual, the sensual body of the virtual worker is not virtual. So I prefer to speak about cognitive proletariat (cognitariat) in order to emphasise the material (I mean physical, psychological, neurological) disease of the workers involved in the net-economy.

Matthew Fuller, 'Bifo/Berardi, interview on 'The Factory of Unhappiness".

The Free Agents – Daniel Pink (2001)

'Legions of Americans, and increasingly citizens of other countries as well, are abandoning one of the Industrial Revolution's most enduring legacies – the "job" – and forging new ways to work. They're becoming self-employed knowledge workers, proprietors of home-based businesses, temps and permatemps, freelancers and e-lancers, independent contractors and independent professionals, micropreneurs and infopreneurs, part-time consultants, interim executives, on-call troubleshooters, and full-time soloists. And many others who hold what are still nominally "jobs" are doing so under terms closer in spirit to free agency than traditional employment. They're telecommuting. They're hopping from company to company. They're forming ventures which are legally their employers, but whose prospects depend largely on their own individual efforts. And they're swapping, or being forced to swap, steady salaries for pay-for-performance agreements that compensate them in commissions, stock options and bonuses. ... to truly understand where the economy is heading, you need to get to know free agents – who they are, what they do, how they work, and why they've made this choice.'

Daniel Pink, *Free Agent Nation*, page 11.

'Diversification – that is, an independent worker spreading her risk across a portfolio of projects, clients, skills, and customers – is the best hedging strategy. ... Today anyone who holds a job and *isn't* looking for a side gig – or crafting a business plan, writing a screen play, or setting up shop on eBay – is out of touch. Moonlighting is a way to diversify your human capital investments – and hedge against the risk of your company collapsing or your job disappearing. ... In some sense, we're all moonlighters, because in every sense, we're all risk managers.'

Daniel Pink, *Free Agent Nation*, page 93.

The Class of the New

The Cybertariat – Ursula Huws (2001)

'... across the ... workforce an extraordinary and unprecedented convergence has been taking place. From tele-sales staff to typesetters, from indexers to insurance underwriters, from librarians to ledger clerks, from planning inspectors to pattern-cutters, a large and increasing proportion of daily work time is spent identically: sitting with one hand poised over a keyboard and the other dancing back and forth from keys to mouse. Facing these workers on the screen, framed in pseudo bas relief, are ugly grey squares labelled, in whatever the local language, "File", "Edit", "View", "Tools", "Format", "Window", or "Help", the ghastly spoor of some aesthetically challenged employee of Microsoft of the late 1980s.'

>Ursula Huws, *The Making of a Cybertariat*, page 165.

'The fact that skills are now generic has made it easier to skip laterally from job to job, company to company, industry to industry. But by the same token each worker has also become more easily dispensable, more easily replaceable; thus the new opportunities also constitute new threats. The combination of this new occupational mobility with the huge expansion of the potential labour pool has also made it much more difficult to build stable group identities based on shared skills. ... Any investment of time and effort in learning a new software package may be wiped out in a matter of months by the launch of a replacement. ... At the head office, e-mail brings senior and junior members of staff into direct communication with one another, cutting out middle layers of management, and a strange new camaraderie develops between colleagues of different grades as one shows the other how to eliminate a virus, or unzip an obstinate attachment. But simultaneously an unbridgeable gulf may have opened up between these same head office staff and their fellow employees at a remote call centre, or data-processing site.'

>Ursula Huws, *The Making of a Cybertariat*, pages 166-167.

The Netocracy – Alexander Bard and Jan Söderqvist (2002)

'In ... [the informational society] a merciless power structure of networks is constructed, in which the most exclusive network, to which only the uppermost netocratic elite has access, is at the top. Family names mean nothing here, unlike under feudalism. Wealth means nothing here, unlike under capitalism. The decisive factor governing where in the hierarchy an individual ends up is instead his or her attentionality: their access to and capacity to absorb, sort, overview, generate the necessary attention for and share valuable information. ...

It is, paradoxically, the netocrats' ability to think beyond their own ego, to build their identity on membership of a group instead of individualism, on electronic tribalism instead of mass-mediated self-assertion, that leads to their understanding and being in control of the new world that is developing. ... Networking itself, the feedback loop and social intelligence are at the very heart of the netocracy.'

Alexander Bard and Jan Söderqvist, *Netocracy*, pages 117-118.

The Precariat - Frassanito Network (2002)

'Precarious work refers to all possible forms of insecure, non-guaranteed flexible exploitation: from illegalised, seasonal and temporary employment to homework, flex-[work] and temp-work, to subcontractors, freelancers, or so-called self-employed persons.

Frassanito Network, 'Precarious, Precarisation, Precariat?', page 60.

'Precariat ... is used as a combative self-description in order to emphasise the subjective and utopian aspects of precarisation. Through the mass refusal of gender roles, of factory work, and of the command of labour over life ... it is possible to speak indeed of flexibilisation from below. Precarisation is not simply an invention of the command centres of capitalism: it is also a reaction to the insurgency and new mobility of living labour, and in this sense it can be understood as the attempt to *recapture* manifold struggles and refusals in order to establish new conditions of [the] exploitation of labour and valorisation of capital.'

Frassanito Network, 'Precarious, Precarisation, Precariat?', page 61.

The Creative Class – Richard Florida (2002)

'This young man [with spiked multi-coloured hair, full-body tattoos, and multiple piercings in his ears] and his lifestyle proclivities represent a profound new force in the economy and life of America. He is a member of what I call the creative class: a fast-growing, highly educated, and well-paid segment of the workforce on whose efforts corporate profits and economic growth increasingly depend. Members of the creative class do a wide variety of work in a wide variety of industries – from technology to entertainment, journalism to finance, high-end manufacturing to the arts. They do not consciously think of themselves as a class. Yet they share a common ethos that values creativity, individuality, difference, and merit.

More and more businesses understand that ethos and are making the adaptations necessary to attract and retain creative class employees – everything from relaxed dress codes, flexible schedules, and new work rules in the office to hiring recruiters who throw Frisbees. Most civic leaders, however, have failed to understand that what is true for corporations is also true for cities and regions: Places that succeed in attracting and retaining creative class people prosper; those that fail don't.'

Richard Florida, 'The Rise of the Creative Class', pages 3-4.

'The distinguishing characteristic of the Creative Class is that its members engage in work whose function is to "create meaningful new forms." I define the Creative Class as consisting of two components. The Super-Creative Core of this new class includes scientists and engineers, university professors, poets and novelists, artists, entertainers, actors, designers, and architects, as well as the thought leadership of modern society: nonfiction writers, editors, cultural figures, think-tank researchers, analysts, and other opinion-makers. ... I define the highest order of creative work as producing new forms or designs that are readily transferable and widely useful – such as designing a product that can be widely made, sold and used; coming up with a theorem or strategy that can be applied in many cases; or composing music that can be performed again and again. ...

Beyond this core group, the Creative Class also includes "creative professionals" who work in a wide range of knowledge-intensive industries such as high-tech sectors, financial services, the legal and healthcare professions, and business management. These people engage in creative problem-solving, drawing on complex bodies of knowledge to solve specific problems. Doing so typically requires a high degree of formal education and thus a high level of human capital. People who do this kind of work ... *are* required to ... think on their own. They apply or combine standard approaches in unique ways to fit the situation, exercise a great deal of judgment, perhaps try something radically new from time to time. ...

Much the same is true of the growing number of technicians and others who apply complex bodies of knowledge to working with physical materials. ... In fields such as medicine and scientific research, technicians are taking on increased responsibility to interpret their work and make decisions, blurring the old distinction between white-collar work (done by decision-makers) and blue-collar work (done by those who follow orders). ...

Everywhere we look, creativity is increasingly valued. Firms and organisations value it for the results that it can produce and individuals value it as a route to self-expression and job satisfaction. Bottom line: As creativity becomes more valued, the Creative Class grows.'

Richard Florida, *The Rise of the Creative Class*, pages 68-71.

The Pro-Ams – Charlie Leadbeater and Paul Miller (2004)

'... in the last two decades a new breed of amateur has emerged: the Pro-Am, amateurs who work to professional standards. ... The Pro-Ams are knowledgeable, educated, committed and networked, by new technology. The twentieth century was shaped by large hierarchical organisations with professionals at the top. Pro-Ams are creating new, distributed organisational models that will be innovative, adaptive and low-cost.'

Charlie Leadbeater and Paul Miller, *The Pro-Am Revolution*, page 12.

'Pro-Ams are not professionals. They do not see themselves that way. They do not earn more than 50 percent of their income from their Pro-

Am activities. ... Yet to call Pro-Ams amateurs is also misleading. ... Many of the defining features of professionalism also apply to Pro-Ams: they have a strong sense of vocation; they use recognised public standards to assess performance and formally validate skills; they form self-regulating communities, which provide people with a sense of community and belonging; they produce non-commodity products and services; they are well versed in a body of knowledge and skill, which carries with it a sense of tradition and identity.'

Charlie Leadbeater and Paul Miller, *The Pro-Am Revolution*, page 22.

'The relationship between amateurs and professional is becoming more fluid and dynamic. It is not a zero-sum game. Professionals and Pro-Ams can grow together.

Pro-Ams work at their leisure, regard consumption as a productive activity and set professional standards to judge their amateur efforts.'

Charlie Leadbeater and Paul Miller, *The Pro-Am Revolution*, page 23.

5.
References

Michel Aglietta, *A Theory of Capitalist Regulation: the US experience*, Verso, London 1979.

Ian Angell, *The New Barbarian Manifesto: how to survive the information age*, Kogan Page, London 2000.

Aristotle, *The Politics*, Penguin, London 1962.

Stanley Aronowitz, 'The Professional-Managerial Class or Middle Strata' in Pat Walker (editor), *Between Labour & Capital*, Harvester, Hassocks 1979, pages 213-242.

Aufheben, 'Keep on Smiling: questions on immaterial labour', *Aufheben*, Number 14, pages 23-44.

Richard Barbrook, 'The Hi-Tech Gift Economy', *First Monday*, Number 12, Volume 3, December 1998, <www.firstmonday.dk/issues/issue3_12/barbrook/index.html>.

Richard Barbrook, 'Cyber-Communism: how the Americans are superseding capitalism in cyberspace', *Science as Culture*, Number 1, Volume 9, 2000, pages 5-40, <www.nettime.org/Lists-Archives/nettime-l-9909/msg00046.html>.

The Class of the New

Richard Barbrook, 'The Regulation of Liberty: free speech, free trade and free gifts on the Net', *Science as Culture*, Number 2, Volume 11, 2002, pages 155-170, <www.constantvzw.com/copy.cult/texts/reg_liberty1.html>.

Richard Barbrook, *Imaginary Futures: from thinking machines to the global village*, Pluto, London forthcoming, <www.imaginaryfutures.net>.

Richard Barbrook and Andy Cameron, 'The Californian Ideology' in Peter Ludlow (editor), *Crypto Anarchy, Cyberstates and Pirate Utopias*, MIT Press, Cambridge Mass 2001, pages 363-387, <www.hrc.wmin.ac.uk/theory-californianideology.html>.

Richard Barbrook and Pit Schultz, 'The Digital Artisans Manifesto', *ZKP 4*, nettime, Ljubljana 1997, pages 52-53, <www.nettime.org/Lists-Archives/nettime/l/9705/msg00120.html>.

Alexander Bard and Jan Söderqvist, *Netocracy: the new power elite and life after capitalism*, Pearson Education, London 2002.

Daniel Bell, *The Coming of Post-Industrial Society: a venture in social forecasting*, Basic Books, New York 1973.

Walter Benjamin, *The Arcades Project*, Harvard University Press, Cambridge Mass 1999.

Sergio Bologna, 'The Tribe of Moles' in Red Notes, *Working Class Autonomy and the Crisis: Italian Marxist texts of the theory and practice of a class movement 1964-79*, Red Notes/CSE, London 1979, pages 67-91.

Harry Braverman, *Labour and Monopoly Capital: the degradation of work in the twentieth century*, Monthly Review Press, New York 1974.

John Brockman, *Digerati: encounters with the cyber elite*, Hardwired, San Francisco 1996.

David Brooks, *Bobos in Paradise: the new upper class and how they got there*, Simon & Schuster, New York 2000.

James Burnham, *The Managerial Revolution*, Penguin, London 1945.

Paul Cardan [Cornelius Castoriadis], *Modern Capitalism and Revolution*, Solidarity, London 1965.

Benjamin Coriat, *L'Atelier et le Robot: essai sur le Fordisme et la production de masse à l'âge de l'électronique*, Christian Bourgeois Éditeur, Paris 1990.

Creative London, *Believe: a manifesto to grow the national GCP (gross creative product)*, LDA, London 2005.

References

Michael Cusumano and David Yoffie, *Competing on Internet Time: lessons from Netscape and its battle against Microsoft*, Free Press, New York 1998.

Ralf Dahrendorf, *Class and Class Conflict in an Industrial Society*, Routledge & Kegan Paul, London 1959.

Gilles Deleuze and Félix Guattari, *A Thousand Plateaus: capitalism and schizophrenia*, Athlone Press, London 1988.

Adolphe d'Ennery and Grangé, 'Les Bohémiens de Paris' in Walter Benjamin, *The Arcades Project*, Harvard University Press, Cambridge Mass 1999, page 428.

Department of Culture, Media and Sports, 'Creative Industries Forum On Intellectual Property Launched', 19th July 2004, <www.culture.gov.uk/global/press_notices/archive_2004/dcms089_04.htm>.

Julian Dibbell, 'We Pledge Allegiance to the Penguin', *Wired*, 12.11, November 2004, <www.wired.com/wired/archive/12.11/linux.html>.

Milovan Djilas, *The New Class*, Unwin, London 1957.

Lucrezia de Domizio Durini, *The Felt Hat: Joseph Beuys - a life told*, Charta, Milan 1997.

Peter Drucker, *The Effective Executive*, Pan, London 1970.

Barbara & John Ehrenreich, 'The Professional-Managerial Class' in Pat Walker (editor), *Between Labour & Capital*, Harvester, Hassocks 1979, pages 5-45.

Elancentric, 'Project Description', <www.demos.co.uk/knowledgebase/research-gateway>.

Richard Florida, *The Rise of the Creative Class: and how it's transforming work, leisure, community and everyday life*, Basic, New York 2002.

Richard Florida, 'The Rise of the Creative Class: why cities without gays and rock bands are losing the economic development race', *Washington Monthly*, May 2002, <www.washingtonmonthly.com/features/2001/0205.florida.html>.

Thomas Frank, *What's The Matter With Kansas?: how conservatives won the heart of America*, Metropolitan, New York 2004.

Friedrich Engels, *The Condition of the Working Class in England*, Basil Blackwell, Oxford 1958.

The Class of the New

Adam Ferguson, *An Essay on the History of Civil Society*, Edinburgh University Press, Edinburgh 1966.

Henry Ford in collaboration with Samuel Crowther, *My Life and Work*, William Heinemann, London 1922.

Frassanito Network, 'Precarious, Precarisation, Precariat?' in *Precarious Reader*, Mute, Volume 2 #0, 2005, pages 60-62.

Matthew Fuller, 'Bifo/Berardi, interview on 'The Factory of Unhappiness'', *nettime*, 11th June 2001, <www.nettime.org/Lists-Archives/nettime-l-0106/msg00033.html>.

John Kenneth Galbraith, *The New Industrial State*, Penguin, London 1969.

John Kenneth Galbraith, *The Affluent Society*, Penguin, London 1970.

Mark Geise, 'From ARPAnet to the Internet: a cultural clash and its implications in framing the debate on the information superhighway' in Lance Strate, Ron Jacobson and Stephanie B. Gibson (editors), *Communications and Cyberspace: social interaction in an electronic environment*, Hampton Press, Cresskill New Jersey 1996, pages 123-141.

George Gilder, *The Spirit of Enterprise*, Penguin, London 1986.

George Gilder, *Wealth and Poverty*, Institute for Contemporary Studies, San Francisco 1993.

GLA Economics, *Creativity: London's Core Business*, Greater London Authority, London 2002, <www.creativelondon.org.uk/upload/pdf/create_inds_rep02_20051025155056.pdf>.

GLC, *The London Industrial Strategy*, Greater London Council, London 1985.

GLC, *The State of the Art or the Art of the State?: strategies for the cultural industries in London*, Greater London Council, London 1985.

Tom Gorman, *Multipreneuring*, Fireside, New York 1996.

André Gorz, *Farewell to the Working Class: an essay on post-industrial socialism*, Pluto, London 1980.

Antonio Gramsci, *Selections From the Prison Notebooks*, Lawrence and Wishart, London 1973.

Miklós Haraszti, *Worker in a Worker's State: piece rates in Hungary*, Penguin, London 1977.

References

Donna Haraway, 'A Cyborg Manifesto: science, technology and socialist-feminism in the late twentieth century', *Simians, Cyborgs and Women: the reinvention of nature*, Free Association Books, London 1991, pages 149-181.

Michael Hauben and Ronda Hauben, *Netizens: on the history and impact of Usenet and the Internet*, IEEE Computer Society Press, Los Alamitos 1997.

Friedrich Hayek, *Individualism and Economic Order*, University of Chicago Press, Chicago 1980.

Georg Hegel, *The Philosophy of Right*, Oxford University Press, Oxford 1967.

Doug Henwood, *After the New Economy: the binge ... and the hangover that won't go away*, The New Press, New York 2005.

Abbie Hoffman, *Woodstock Nation: a talk-rock album*, Vintage, New York 1969.

Ursula Huws, *The Making of a Cybertariat: virtual work in a real world*, Monthly Review, New York 2003.

Muhammad Ibn Khaldûn, *The Muqaddimah: an introduction to history*, Princeton University Press, Princeton 1969.

Anthony Iles and Benedict Seymour, 'The (Re)Occupation', *Mute*, 5 January 2006, <www.metamute.org/en/The-Re-Occupation>.

Humphrey Jennings, *Pandaemonium: the coming of the machine as seen by contemporary observers*, Picador, London 1985.

Jon Katz, 'The Digital Citizen', *Wired*, 5.12, December 1997, pages 68-82, 274-275.

Karl Kautsky, *The Class Struggle*, W.W. Norton, New York 1971.

Kevin Kelly, *New Rules for the New Economy: 10 ways that the network economy is changing everything*, Fourth Estate, London 1998.

Michael Kelly, *White-Collar Proletarians: the industrial behaviour of British civil servants*, Routledge & Kegan Paul, London 1980.

Clark Kerr, John Dunlop, Frederick Harbison and Charles Myers, *Industrialism and Industrial Man: the problems of labour and management in economic growth*, Heinemann, London 1962.

Arthur Kroker and Michael Weinstein, *Data Trash: the theory of the virtual class*, New World Perspectives, Montreal 1994.

The Class of the New

Hari Kunzru, 'A Dispatch from Tony's Café: the anti-gentrification struggle on Broadway Market', *The Guardian*, 5th January 2006, <www.guardian.co.uk/g2/story/0,,1678046,00.html>.

Maurizio Lazzarato, 'General Intellect: towards an inquiry into immaterial labour', *Ed Emery, His Archive*, <www.emery.archive.mcmail.com/public_html/immaterial/lazzarat.html>.

Charlie Leadbeater and Kate Oakley, *The Independents: Britain's new cultural entrepreneur*, Demos, London 1999.

Charlie Leadbeater and Paul Miller, *The Pro-Am Revolution: how enthusiasts are changing our economy and our society*, Demos, London 2004.

Henri Lefebvre, *Everyday Life in the Modern World*, Transaction, New Brunswick 1984.

V.I. Lenin, *Imperialism: the highest stage of capitalism*, Communist Party of Great Britain, London 1928.

V.I. Lenin, *What Is To Be Done?*, Foreign Languages Press, Peking 1975.

Rick Levine, Christopher Locke, Doc Searls and David Weinberger, *The Cluetrain Manifesto: the end of business as usual*, Perseus, Cambridge Mass 2000.

Steven Levy, *Hackers: heroes of the computer revolution*, Penguin, London 1984.

Alain Lipietz, *Towards a New Economic Order: post-Fordism, ecology and democracy*, Polity, Cambridge 1992.

Ken Livingstone, *If Voting Changed Anything, They'd Abolish It*, Fontana, London 1987.

Jean-François Lyotard, *The Post-Modern Condition: a report on knowledge*, Manchester University Press, Manchester 1986.

Maureen Mackintosh and Hilary Wainwright, *A Taste of Power: the politics of local economics*, Verso, London 1987.

Gautam Malkani, 'Look Beyond the Media Heartlands for the Full Story', Special Report: Creative Business, *Financial Times*, 29th November 2005, pages 6-7.

Serge Mallet, *The New Working Class*, Spokesman, Nottingham 1975.

Ernest Mandel, *Late Capitalism*, Verso, London 1978.

Karl Marx, *Grundrisse*, Penguin, London 1973.

References

Karl Marx, *Capital Volume 1: a critique of political economy*, Penguin, London 1976.

Karl Marx, *Capital Volume 3: a critique of political economy*, Penguin/New Left Review, London 1981.

Karl Marx and Friedrich Engels, *The Communist Manifesto*, Lawrence & Wishart, London 1983.

Bethany McLean and Peter Elkind, *The Smartest Guys in the Room: the amazing rise and scandalous fall of Enron*, Portfolio, New York 2004.

Ludwig von Mises, *Human Action: a treatise on economics*, Contemporary Books, Chicago 1966.

William Morris, 'Socialism and Politics (An Answer to 'Another View')', *Political Writings: contributions to Justice and Commonwealth 1883-1890*, Thoemmes, Bristol 1994, pages 98-100.

William Morris, 'Socialism From the Root Up', *Political Writings: contributions to Justice and Commonwealth 1883-1890*, Thoemmes, Bristol 1994, pages 495-622.

John Naisbitt, *Megatrends: ten new directions transforming our lives*, Futura, London 1984.

Antonio Negri, 'Keynes and the Capitalist Theories of the State Post-1929', *Revolution Retrieved: selected writings on Marx, Keynes, capitalist crisis & new social subjects 1967-83*, Red Notes, London 1988, pages 9-42.

Antonio Negri, 'The Crisis of the Crisis-State', *Revolution Retrieved: selected writings on Marx, Keynes, capitalist crisis & new social subjects 1967-83*, Red Notes, London 1988, pages 177-197.

Antonio Negri, 'Archaeology and Project: the mass worker and the social worker', *Revolution Retrieved: selected writings on Marx, Keynes, capitalist crisis & new social subjects 1967-83*, Red Notes, London 1988, pages 199-230.

Antonio Negri and Michael Hardt, *Empire*, Harvard University Press, Cambridge Mass, 2000.

Friedrich Nietzsche, *Thus Spoke Zarathustra: a book for everyone and no one*, Penguin, London 1961.

Friedrich Nietzsche, *The Will to Power*, Vintage, New York 1968.

George Orwell, *Nineteen Eighty-Four: a novel*, Penguin, London 1954.

The Class of the New

David Panos, 'Create Creative Clusters', *Mute*, Number 28, Summer/Autumn 2004, pages 6-8, <www.metamute.com/look/article.tpl?IdLanguage=1&IdPublication=1&NrIssue=28&NrSection=10&NrArticle=1379>.

Tom Peters and Robert Waterman, *In Search of Excellence: lessons from America's best run companies*, Harper & Row, New York 1982.

Mario Piazzesi, 'The *Squadristi* as the Revolutionaries of the New Italy' in Roger Griffen (editor), *Fascism*, Oxford University Press, Oxford 1995, pages 39-40.

Décio Pignatari, *Contracomunicacao*, Editora Perspectiva, São Paulo 1971.

Daniel Pink, *Free Agent Nation: how America's independent workers are transforming the way we live*, Time Warner, New York 2001.

Nicos Poulantzas, *Classes in Contemporary Capitalism*, NLB, London 1975.

Robert Reich, *The Work of Nations: preparing ourselves for 21st-century capitalism*, Simon & Schuster, London 1991.

Jonas Ridderstråle and Kjell Nordström, *Funky Business: talent makes capital dance*, ft.com, London 2000.

Jerry Rubin, *Do It!: scenarios of the revolution*, Simon and Schuster, New York 1970.

Henri Saint-Simon, 'Comparison Between the National (Industrial) Party and the Anti-National Party', *Selected Writings on Science, Industry and Social Organisation*, Holmes and Meier, New York 1975, pages 187-191.

Henri Saint-Simon, 'A Political Parable', *Selected Writings on Science, Industry and Social Organisation*, Holmes and Meier, New York 1975, pages 194-197.

Raphael Samuel, 'The Workshop of the World: steam power and hand technology in mid-Victorian Britain', *History Workshop: a journal of socialist historians*, Issue 3, Spring 1977, pages 6-72.

Joseph Schumpeter, *Capitalism, Socialism and Democracy*, Harper, New York 1976.

Benedict Seymour, 'Shoreditch and the Creative Destruction of the Inner City', *The London Particular*, <www.thelondonparticular.org/items/creativedestruction.html>.

Samuel Smiles, *Self-Help: with illustrations of conduct and perseverance*, IEA, London 1996.

References

Adam Smith, *An Inquiry into the Nature and Causes of the Wealth of Nations Volume 1 & Volume 2*, University of Chicago Press, Chicago 1976.

Frederick Winslow Taylor, *The Principles of Scientific Management*, W.W. Norton, New York 1967.

Alvin Toffler, *The Third Wave*, Pan, London 1981.

Alain Touraine, *The Post-Industrial Society: tomorrow's social history – classes, conflicts and culture in the programmed society*, Wildwood House, London 1974.

Thorstein Veblen, *The Engineers and the Price System*, Transaction, New Brunswick 1983.

Carlo Vercellone, 'Sens et Enjeux de la Transition vers le Capitalisme Cognitif: une mise en perspective historique', *Immaterial Labour, Multitudes and New Social Subjects: class composition in cognitive capitalism*, <www.geocities.com/immateriallabour/vercellone-capitalisme-cognitif.html>.

Max Weber, *Essays in Sociology*, Routledge & Kegan Paul, London 1948.

H.G. Wells, *The Open Conspiracy: blueprints for a world revolution*, Victor Gollancz, London 1928.

H.G. Wells, *A Modern Utopia*, House of Stratus, New York 2002.

William Whyte, *The Organisation Man*, Penguin, London 1960.

Thomas Wright (the Journeyman Engineer), *The Great Unwashed*, Augustus M. Kelley, New York, 1970.

C. Wright Mills, *White Collar: the American middle classes*, Oxford University Press, New York 1951.

C. Wright Mills, *The Power Elite*, Oxford University Press, New York 1956.

Gregory Zinoviev, 'The Social Roots of Opportunism', *New International*, Number 2, Winter 1983-84, pages 97-143.

Shoshana Zuboff, *In the Age of the Smart Machine: the future of work and power*, Heinemann, Oxford 1988.

Printed in the United Kingdom
by Lightning Source UK Ltd.
111021UKS00001B/415-597